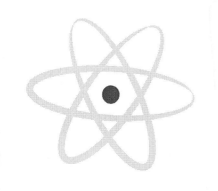

PREACHING

Maybe It *Is* Rocket Science

JAMES T. BRADFORD

Gospel Publishing House
Springfield, Missouri
02-0482

Scripture quotations taken from The Holy Bible, New International Version®. NIV®. Copyright © 1973, 1978, 1984, 2011 by Biblica, Inc.™ Used by permission. All rights reserved worldwide.

The "NIV" and "New International Version" are trademarks registered in the United States Patent and Trademark Office by Biblica, Inc.™

Scripture quotations marked (NASB®) are taken from the New American Standard Bible®, Copyright © 1960, 1962, 1963, 1968, 1971, 1972, 1973, 1975, 1977, 1995 by The Lockman Foundation. Used by permission. (www.Lockman.org <http://www.Lockman.org>)

KJV refers to the King James Version of the Bible.

© 2011 by Gospel Publishing House, 1445 N. Boonville Ave., Springfield, Missouri 65802. No part of this book may be reproduced, stored in a retrieval system, or transmitted in any form or by any means—electronic, mechanical, photocopy, recording, or otherwise—without prior written permission of the copyright owner, except brief quotations used in connection with reviews in magazines or newspapers. All rights reserved.

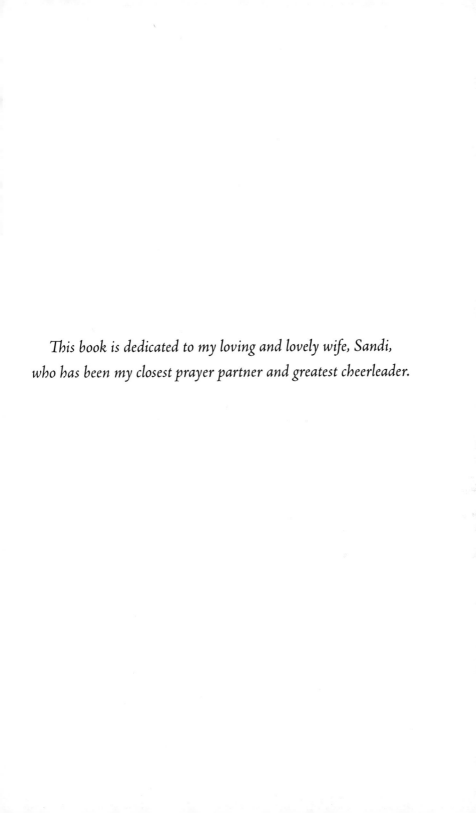

*This book is dedicated to my loving and lovely wife, Sandi,
who has been my closest prayer partner and greatest cheerleader.*

Contents

Foreword

I love to hear Jim Bradford preach. In the many times I've listened to him, I've never heard him preach a "bad" sermon. Why is that? Why are his messages so good? It's because he bathes his sermons in prayer, preparation, and passion.

I kid Jim about being a rocket scientist; his PhD from the University of Minnesota is in aerospace engineering. His scientific training means he approaches study with a disciplined mind. You know when you hear him that he's done his homework on the Scripture text and carefully applied that text to everyday life.

I once went into a pastor's study, and the few volumes in his library were titled *Simple Simon Sermon Outlines*. You won't find those books in Dr. Bradford's library. His sermons are easy to grasp but not simplistic. I think of his preaching in terms of John 1:1–18—the prologue of John's Gospel. Almost all the words in this passage have one or two syllables. They are simple enough for a child to understand, but the depth of those words speaks powerfully to the most educated and disciplined mind as well. I've watched people from every walk of life and age group listen to Jim with rapt attention as he preaches. The Holy Spirit takes his thoroughly prepared message and distributes it to each life.

But preparation is powerless without prayer. If there's just one thing you can say about Jim Bradford it is that he is a man of God. I watch him as he worships during the song service, one step forward, right arm raised, voice lifted to God. Whether in public or in private, he is a pray-er. When I listen to him preach, I have confidence that he has wrestled through the preparation of his message with prayer.

Added to the prayer and preparation is Jim's passion for the Word. I've never heard him minister without passion—passion for God, for the moving of His Spirit, and for people and their needs.

If you want those same qualities in increasing measure in your own life, then take time to read this book. It will warm your heart, enrich your mind, and help you be a more effective preacher of God's Word!

George O. Wood
General Superintendent of the Assemblies of God

Acknowledgements

Thank you to my wife, Sandi, for her loving support and constant commitment to following the call of God on our lives. Over the years her constructive reflections and encouragements have helped to shape me as a preacher. I also appreciate her wisdom in waiting until Wednesdays to critique the messages from Sunday!

Thank you as well to Randy Hurst, without whom this book would not have been possible. I deeply appreciate the hours that he and his team have taken to distill down our lengthy interviews into structure and script. I am also indebted to Randy for the very affirming and loyal friend he has been to me personally.

Finally, thank you to Dr. George Wood, who has penned the foreword to this book. For years he has been a highly valued friend, mentor, and encourager. I am indebted to him for his support, confidence, and role-modeling. It is one of the great honors of my life to serve on his team.

Introduction

You've probably heard the expression, "It isn't rocket science." This statement implies that, whatever the topic, it's something easy or simple to do. The statement shouldn't be made about preaching. Preaching isn't easy, or even simple for that matter. It is hard work and requires time.

Wherever I have pastored, people have been aware of my academic background. The youth of my last pastorate, Central Assembly in Springfield, Missouri, used it creatively. To invite their fellow students to church, they had bright green T-shirts made. The front read "Central Assembly" and the back read, "My pastor is a rocket scientist." It was a good conversation starter, I suppose, and possibly some students visited Central Assembly as a result.

A significant component of Central Assembly's congregation is preachers. Some have commented to me that the nontraditional structure of my messages helped them gain insights into the Word and make life applications.

What does all this have to do with preaching? I was encouraged to write this book by a couple of those preachers in my congregation at Central.

Because I came into preaching ministry through a different route than most, possibly my experience can provide some fresh insights that will help you "excel still more" (1 Thessalonians 4:1, NASB) in your preaching.

Growing up, I found myself oriented academically more toward the sciences rather than humanities, literature, and psychology, things I would need in ministry. I really like numbers. I like the tangible character of the physical sciences. I was fascinated by light, by space travel—by those romantic things that are associated with aerospace engineering, my field of study. I attended the University of Minnesota, which is a research school more than a design school. I took five years of calculus. We studied the flow of fluids under rotation. Fluid mechanics, the study of the flow of liquids and gases, is one of the aerospace fields.

I was very challenged by an exceptionally gifted fluid mechanics teacher when I went on to graduate school. He had been chief engineer at Union Carbide. He was a phenomenal communicator. Later, he was named teacher of the year at the Institute of Technology, University of Minnesota. I learned a lot more than engineering listening to his lectures. He was systematic. He was clear. His fluid mechanics lectures embodied the best of what I later learned to appreciate in a good sermon. There wasn't frustrating extraneous stuff where you just get lost. The linearity of his lectures unfolded like a story. And the deeper he'd get into the lecture and the more panels on the blackboard he'd fill up with notes, the more excited he'd get because an emerging awareness was unfolding that could be followed easily from beginning to end.

That's the mystery of every message you want to preach.

Something begins unfolding, even if it's not point one, point two, point three. There's a storyline built around the linear direction of your message as it unfolds. And I experienced that listening to him. When I was about to finish undergraduate school, he asked me if I would go on contract with him as a research assistant, which I did for the full five years that I was in graduate school. Our research focused on rotating fluid flows, similar to what we find in the atmosphere or inside centrifuges. The title of my PhD dissertation was "The Nongeostrophic Baroclinic Instability of Two Fluids," referring to rotational fluid flows that have frictional shear forces applied to them. With some very long calculus equations, we mathematically predicted where the instabilities would occur and then verified those predictions experimentally.

Because the Aerospace Department was more "research" than "applied" in its orientation, we did not actually design aircraft or spaceships. Instead we simply added a little more to the body of scientific literature concerning nongeostrophic baroclinic flows.

We published in a couple of scientific fluid mechanics journals and left it to other scientists around the world to actually apply our work to real-life engineering situations.

(Just a thought—I eventually found out that "proposition" without "application" doesn't work well with preaching, but you can get by with it in the scientific world.)

Engineering has helped me think systematically and that created a framework for preaching ministry. The engineer in me is used to flow charts and sequenced tasks. I've learned to structure a message from beginning to end and see that sequence. People tell me that the linear characteristic of engineering helps me communicate in a manner an audience can follow.

Engineering helps me to identify key points when I study a Scripture passage. As a result, outlines come to me with some ease; after all, outlines need to have a logical sense to them. Engineering taught me to interpret data, and I use those interpretive lessons when identifying a central thread in a passage of Scripture. To develop a hypothesis in science, you must develop a theory that ties together and explains all the pieces of data you have gathered. The engineer in me regularly asks, "What's the central thing the Holy Spirit is saying that connects all the pieces in this passage of Scripture?"

I have learned to balance the value of other people's contributions to the body of scriptural knowledge with my own need for the personal, hard work of Scripture study. The scientist who builds on others' research must still develop his or her own data and results. In ministry, if you rely too heavily on somebody else's material, you won't adequately nourish your congregation. I regularly ask myself, "What is God saying to this congregation? What has God been doing in our community?"

Engineering helps me remain true to the biblical text, to the truth data God has bequeathed to us. I find that some preaching is not authentically biblical. Some ministers fail to apply the original intended meaning of the Scripture. They lose sight of the context and pick a word or a phrase to which they react and through which they feel inspired; but that piece of the text, when torn out and shared in isolation, may have nothing to do with the central thread of that paragraph or chapter.

My engineering instincts prod me to discover why this paragraph of Scripture is here and what it is intended to say as a central truth. Without that discipline, I might just as easily use Scripture as a platform to say what I want to say rather than saying what Scripture actually says.

A scientist finds great satisfaction when theories translate into real-life benefits. Similarly, as a pastor, my most satisfying experience is when people really open up Scripture and interact with the text and with me throughout the sermon to see that passage unfold. That experience validates every step of preparation.

If you haven't studied and discovered for yourself how a passage unfolds—the central thread, how it develops, the sequence of thought—you will be ill-equipped to invite your congregation on a similar journey.

Decades now after my doctoral studies, my engineering persona continues to afford me ministry tools. As I outline the sequence of thought in a passage, as I rephrase it and restate what's in black and white in the text, as I put arrows here and there to show how thoughts connect and their sequence, my sermon preparation begins to look a bit like a flow chart. I can see the patterns. I know I'm treating Scripture seriously. I know that when I preach I'll be ready to unfold what the passage authentically says.

I share all of the above not to convince you to apply to Berkeley, MIT, or Virginia Tech as a needed supplement to your Bible school or seminary training. Rather, God directed my learning in such a way that what might appear to others as a pragmatic skill set has been used by the Holy Spirit to shape my life and resource my ministry. If I can share with you in the following pages some of those principles, I believe the Holy Spirit can help you adapt them in your ministry to the best possible use.

Perhaps you picked up this book out of a slight sense of desperation. You feel overwhelmed and underassisted. I'm convinced if your congregation is to grow, your people need to allow you to spend time differently in two areas. One is in more leadership development, so you are doing ministry increasingly *through* people rather than *to* people. And the other is spending more time on your Sunday morning message.

I can't change the dynamics of your congregation, but perhaps in these few chapters I can communicate some of the benefits of healthy sermon preparation. My prayer for you is that God will encourage you and empower you to feed His Word to His flock and then multiply your ministry among them. As Scripture comes alive in your life and in your congregation, I know you will soon identify new ministry partners sitting in those pews. Together, you will more powerfully reach out to your community and to our world.

1 Four Resources for Equipping Saints

Nothing compares to that sense of connecting with God, connecting with His Word, and connecting with His people.

All Scripture is God-breathed and is useful for teaching, rebuking, correcting and training in righteousness, so that the servant of God may be thoroughly equipped for every good work (2 Timothy 3:16,17).

Second Timothy 3:16,17 is a remarkable passage, assuring us in conjunction with other points of Scripture that God's Spirit and God's Word always work together. Ephesians 6:17 tells us to use "the sword of the Spirit, which is the word of God." The presence of God's Word acts as a spiritual force of gravity drawing in the activity of the Holy Spirit. I view the Holy Spirit as a flame and God's Word as the fuel. And they always work together.

We must start the preaching task from a steadfast conviction of the inspiration of Scripture, as this passage so powerfully proclaims: "All Scripture is God-breathed." When we accept God's Word as His planned communication to establish His intended relationship with mankind, we understand that life-change happens through people's exposure to the Word of God.

A friend of mine, who served as the U.S. president of Wycliffe International, told me, "Everywhere we've translated Scriptures into a local dialect where they had never had the Scripture in their language before, there's a church today."

God's Spirit always works through His Word. The apostle Paul presents four ways the Spirit uses God's Word: teaching, rebuking, correcting and training. And the pastor has the privilege and responsibility of partnering with the Spirit in each of those tasks. My shorthand descriptions of those pastoral responsibilities are:

+ Teaching—what we need to believe
+ Rebuking—what we need to stop doing
+ Correcting—what we need to start doing
+ Training—what we need to become

God's Word accomplishes all four of these. It is the pastor's task to ensure that all four purposes of the Word come to life in his or her preaching. Personality, ministry philosophy, insecurities and fears can shape this mix, sometimes overemphasizing or excluding an element to the detriment of the congregation. It's easy for a pastor to tend to gravitate to just one or two of these.

For instance, for some preachers, almost every sermon boils down to a rebuke. "Stop sinning!" "God barely loves you!" They may not say such things that bluntly, but they neglect to do the hard work of moving beyond the rebuke to the equally essential elements of correcting and training. They truncate their message without offering good application. Some of us grew up on preaching that was pretty much "Jesus is going to come again, and you probably aren't going to be ready." If you're going to have a balanced diet of God's Word in your church with an accurate view of God, yourself, and the world around you, people need much more than rebuking.

These four divine functions of Scripture serve as a helpful guide to ensure balance in every sermon or series of sermons.

Teaching—What We Need to Believe

The Greek word Paul uses for teaching has to do with doctrine, with substance, with what we need to believe. Many have assumed that the fundamental teaching of doctrine is unpopular at best and irrelevant at worst. In my upbringing in the church, I don't remember the teaching of doctrine having a positive connotation. But the content of Scripture should always be the baseline for everything being worked out in the life of the believer.

I've seen firsthand the toxic effects when one's theology becomes a little bit off. It affects everything else in someone's life. For example, if our Christology is insufficient, people aren't given clear reasons to believe that Jesus is the Son of God or that He really rose from the dead. If our understanding of the kingdom of God is lacking, we lose sight of the rule of God in our life and how that affects all we are and do. Without a clear understanding of Scripture's content, we will lead distracted, valueless lives plagued by misplaced priorities.

While I was pastoring University Church in Minneapolis, some of our young adults were involved with parachurch organizations that operated on subtle deviations from biblical truth. They cast doubt on the fallen nature of man and attributed solely to human choice the ability to love and serve God or self. As a pastor, I could look at such teachings on the surface and say, "Well, I don't know if that is exactly right, but we'll let it pass." But inevitably, I saw that the cumulative effect of those small deviations from truth resulted in broken lives. I had to help put spiritually broken lives back together after people came out of these organizations. There was so much emphasis on human performance that, at best, they constantly felt defeated by guilt and uncertain of their salvation.

Then there were organizations that interpreted biblical authority in wrong ways. Students were taught that to disagree with a leader was evidence of a rebellious spirit. Authority is in Scripture, and obedience is in Scripture, but if they aren't kept in the right tension and balance with things like grace and freedom, people will be hurt spiritually.

For me it was an epiphany, "I get it!" What you believe really does affect how you live, how you look at God, how you look at the world around you, how you look at yourself, and how you feel about reality. What you believe is vital for your whole worldview, your self-identity, and your understanding of your mission.

Teaching the content of Scripture, then, gives the believers under your care a framework within which they establish their whole belief system. And such teaching necessarily involves story narrative as well as doctrinal exposition. The stories are foundational to the doctrine. Nothing beats a balanced diet of the totality of Scripture. You simply must know the stories in Scripture that are the bedrock of biblical doctrine. Sometimes we consign things to Sunday School that need to be brought to life from behind the pulpit—the story of Abraham, Sarah and Isaac; the story of Moses, the Israelites and the Red Sea; the story of David and Goliath; the story of Jonah and the big fish. Think of the Gospels' united story of Jesus and the story of the Early Church in the Book of Acts—I am constantly reading about Jesus and examining His life closely, as well as Acts, because that's the story of Jesus' continuing work through the Church. These are pinnacle stories that are a part of the overarching story of God's saving work.

As preachers, we are visiting the stories and letters and sermons that are in Scripture. Pure biblical content must be the framework by which we look at everything in our life and understand everything in our world. Our sermons cannot rest upon our own stories; we must communicate the Bible's stories. We ask the popular question, "What would Jesus do?" But a knowledge of Scripture lets us ask and discover, "What did Jesus do?" What is the Spirit doing in the New Testament as I study Acts? What do real letters to real churches say about real issues that have parallels to my life and ministry?

Some have tried to create a dichotomy between narrative and didactic Scripture. The Bible is a story. If I could reduce the whole Bible to one sentence, it would be this: It's the story of the God who created us also acting to rescue us. That story unfolds in all kinds of little stories. I'm convinced every page of Scripture will answer one of three questions: What is God like? What am I like as a human being? How can God and I relate? It is never "Sunday Schoolish" or anti-intellectual or a violation of hermeneutic principles or exegetical approaches to give due attention to the Bible's stories. They are in the text for a reason. They are intended to communicate to the people of God and to a lost world specific truths about God, about human nature, and about how the two are supposed to relate.

Rebuking—What We Need to Stop Doing

The transition from teaching to rebuking is difficult for some preachers. I believe you must do the necessary homework in your own heart if your rebuke is going to accomplish what the Spirit intends. I have seen some ministers rebuke, supposedly from a scriptural premise, and yet I've sensed there is more unresolved anger in them than the pure conviction of the Holy Spirit. You must be very careful whenever you prophetically rebuke that you are doing it in the right spirit and that you have dealt with your own issues first.

Never try to solve pastoral problems with individuals from behind the pulpit. That is a misuse of the authority given to the leader of a church. You have the pulpit; you have the platform. The people out there do not. When you start using the pulpit to target individuals, you have shifted from a motive of ministry to one of personal satisfaction. You must take care never to rebuke in the wrong way.

However, Scripture is full of warnings to stop doing things because they are destructive. There is no denying that there are things we need to stop doing. Unfortunately, we live in a "love me but do not judge me" culture. It is an error to rebuke people because of our own issues; it is just as wrong, for the sake of relevance and "loving" people and not building up walls, to avoid or even minimize a vitally needed rebuke.

An expository approach can contribute to the balance and effectiveness of a rebuke. You are simply and honestly communicating the warnings in Scripture. With passages that hold a strong rebuke, I make a point to hold closely to the text. Once in a while I'll say something like, "You know, these are the exact words of Jesus. This may reinforce your worst stereotypes about preachers, but you are not dealing with me. You are dealing with what Jesus said here."

There are plenty of days in my own walk of faith and study of Christ's teaching that Jesus blesses me; there are other days when Jesus bothers me. When I am rebuked by my study of the Word, it bothers me. But I must still reckon with the truth. It's not that God doesn't love me. And I have to take that same understanding into my sermons and help the listeners reconcile the fact that when they are rebuked by God's truth, He still loves them.

Our culture's disintegrating families and poor parenting models complicate this task. People can't reconcile love and rebuke when they come from a shaky home environment. For too many people, love means I get to do anything I want. Rebuke means I have abusive parents who really didn't love me. Parents who always tell their child what they are doing wrong and how bad they are do not offer godly rebuke. Rebuking is not shaming people; if we stay close to the text of Scripture, that allows us to offer restorative rebuke and protects us from destructive shame.

Shaming people falsely defines who they are fundamentally. Shame says, "You are a lousy person. You are an unworthy, unlovable person. You are a failure." Godly rebuke applies divine truth to the things people do. It doesn't cross over to make a person feel unlovable. Godly rebuke reminds people that, because they are loved by God, the things they do must change. So many people deal with a shame-based reality when they receive a rebuke in the family or on the job. If we are not intentional in our application of godly rebuke, they are going to walk out of our churches saying, "I guess I am a lousy person. Pastor reminded me of that again today."

Another advantage to offering serious sequential teaching through Scripture is that it helps us avoid elevating our hobbyhorses. When it comes to rebuking people, we all have those pet sins we tend to magnify. Unfortunately, our favorite things we address in rebuking ways will sometimes betray us. Sometimes we preach hardest against the things we struggle with most personally. We have to be very, very careful.

I tell people all the time my biggest problem is not a church budget or any other daily complication or pressure of ministry; the biggest problem I must deal with is my own heart. Have I done painfully honest work with my own heart first of all? Is what I communicate to others coming out of the counsel of Scripture, or am I just trying to do personal therapy on myself in front of an audience? Sometimes we get on one or two issues, and we're constantly pounding our people on those issues. Eventually, people start looking back at us and say to themselves, "What's your problem with that issue?"

Correcting—What We Need to Start Doing

We teach. We rebuke. We must also correct. The word in the Greek here means to straighten, to go from crooked to straight. I like to look at that as the good things we start to do to replace the wrong things we have stopped doing. Rebuking means you need to stop doing something. But we are not to remain in some vacuum of action. God doesn't call us to live in inertia. Correction from Scripture lets us chart a new course. It's a very positive thing. The correction we offer biblically will help people in a practical way to answer the questions, "How do I believe differently? How do I think differently? How do I relate to people differently? How do I apply the Scripture to help me live Christ's way?" Everything about preaching is life-change in the direction of looking more and more like Jesus, becoming more and more Christlike, more and more open to Him, more and more in conformity with His will for us, more and more like Him in our character and in our values, and more and more obedient to Him.

Jesus is the example. Jesus is the target. Christlikeness is the end of it all. Until we receive biblical correction, we're kind of out on the fringes of the Christian life, meandering around, directionless. But the Scriptures put Christlikeness as the destination. The Greek word for correction means "straighten out the path" and head in a cohesive direction.

I think sometimes, as pastors, we've not thought enough about this. If somebody listens to me preach for five years, what do I want them to look like after those five years? I have to preach from the beginning with the end in mind. My long-term vision for that person will affect the way I structure messages today. I'm not just preaching to nurture and develop my own spiritual gift. People aren't sitting in the service each week to give me an opportunity to polish my oratory or public image. I'm preaching because people out there have overwhelming needs and are grappling with issues of eternal importance. My assignment as a servant is to equip them and to lift them up.

Paul points to this purpose of the Word at the end of 2 Timothy 3:17 when he says that the Scriptures thoroughly equip us for every good work. If I am partnering with the Holy Spirit to maximize the impact of the Word on the life of every person attending my church, then my job is to help cut paths, straight paths, towards Christlikeness out of the text and encourage people to take the next practical steps toward that goal. I'm not laying burdens on them; I'm not expecting them to suddenly run a marathon. I'm walking through the truths of Scripture with them and helping them to identify how to take the next key step that next week, to give them something that will help them begin to think differently, believe differently, act differently. The Scriptures are a great counseling manual. The Scriptures are a great coaching manual. The Scriptures are a great guide for lifestyle decisions and relationships. God's Word is just filled with fantastic truth about the choices we make, the values we have, the direction in which we are heading, and the character that is formed in us.

When I talk to pastors about shaping the lives and choices of their congregations, I readily admit it can be a two-way process. I remember a time when I felt I had plateaued in ministry. I asked our church leadership to develop a sermon evaluation committee whose members represented the congregation I was speaking to. That committee included a high school girl, an eighty-three-year-old grandma, a college professor and his wife, a young couple with little kids, a young couple with teenagers, and a fifty-three-year-old single mom. It was a cross-section of the people who listened to me every week. They had a little sheet that they would fill out after every sermon. It would answer questions such as, "What is the purpose of the message? What is the central theme of the message? What helped you hear this message well? What would have helped you hear this message better?" (That last question was painful.) The committee members would fill that sheet out, and once every three weeks we would meet for an hour and a half on Sunday afternoon. During the first forty-five minutes, we would review the previous three Sunday morning sermons; they returned their sheets to me right after every message. It's not a fun experience saying, "Okay, talk to me," and then closing your mouth. They could say anything they wanted to evaluate my sermons. But it really helped me. They would say, "Sometimes your introductions are too long" or "The central purpose wasn't clear to me."

The second half of that hour-and-a-half meeting, I'd go over the text of the next three sermons. I wasn't asking them to write the sermons for me, but I felt I had been losing touch with the questions people ask when they read certain passages of the Scriptures. Sometimes, after you're preaching for a few years and you're buried in your biblical library, you can become detached from the way your congregation interacts with the Word. I needed to know what a sixteen-year-old girl sitting in my congregation asked when she read a passage, what a single mom asked when she read that passage. Those Sunday afternoon critiques became great Bible studies. The committee members would give me their insights. They'd let me know, "Every time I read this passage, this confuses me." Sometimes I hadn't even thought of the questions and challenges they raised. Our committee met every three weeks for a year. The unanticipated positive spin-off was that every one of the members said, "No one ever taught us how to listen to sermons. This taught us how to listen to sermons."

But the benefit was much more for me.

Training—What We Need to Become

Training takes correction a step further. Training looks beyond new actions to the idea of personal transformation, of becoming. We teach for what we need to believe; we rebuke for what we need to stop doing; we correct for what we need to start doing. But in training, we identify what we need to become.

The Greek word has the idea of nurturing. This is what you do with a child if you are a parent. You train them up. You nurture them. Perhaps you are a mentor to a novice in your profession or a younger Christian in your local body of believers. You're training them. You're mentoring them. You're nurturing them. You're helping them to become everything God has called them to become.

I think it's tragic if we, as preachers, don't have a deep conviction of the God-given potential of every human being who listens to us. In fact, as a pastor, I find it hard just to pray for people's present needs today. I certainly do that; but as a pastor, I'm always interested in not only what they need now, but also what they are going to become tomorrow. When I speak to other pastors I tell them, on any given day, in a sense, I'm pastoring two churches—the church that is here now and the church that will be here ten years from now. In some ways, in regard to every person who listens to me preach, I'm preaching to two people—the person who is sitting there today with their present needs, but also the person they are going to become five or ten years from now.

Every person is becoming. That truth permeates everything I believe about people and the reason that I preach to them. As a preacher of God's Word, I am like a spiritual parent. I'm applying God's Word to their life, progressively forming and shaping whole people out of those truths. Every week we should pray, "Lord, let this be a life-changing sermon." I don't know if someone's life can change every week, but over time the cumulative effect of the full counsel of God's Word helps people to become. It equips them to every good work. It's not so much, "Learn how to stop breaking the rules and learn how to start keeping the rules." It has to be, "Learn how to live a whole life in the fellowship of the Holy Spirit in a comprehensive way where you are actually becoming a better person."

When I was pastoring in Southern California, I had a young professional say to me, "You know, I was thinking about church the other day. I thought, where else can you go in our culture every week and be exposed to a great encouraging message about how you can live better? Where else do you ever get that? Every week, we're constantly getting what we need and being encouraged to be better people, to be better husbands, to be better fathers, to be better in the workplace, to be more open to the Holy Spirit."

That was a powerfully encouraging endorsement of what I was prayerfully seeking to accomplish. His statement really struck me because that describes the process of becoming and growing. That can't be quantified in one Sunday, but the cumulative effect will carry your people on a journey to Christlikeness.

One Pastor's Journey

I have only been able to invest myself in others' lives because so many elders in the faith invested in me. My pastor when I was growing up was H. H. Barber who pastored Calvary Temple in Winnipeg, Manitoba, Canada, one of the prominent evangelical voices in the country. He was very much an orator—a powerful expositional Bible preacher. His ministry shaped my formative years. I did not grow up hearing people abuse Scripture, or reading a verse and connecting it with a bunch of hokey stories and a lame concluding prayer.

In college, my engineering training taught me to picture things in flow charts and outlines. When I was in campus ministry my freshman year with Intervarsity Christian Fellowship, I was taught to do inductive Bible study. You took a sheet of paper, turned it sideways, and drew two lines to make three columns. At the top of each column, you wrote, "What does it say?" "What does it mean?" and "What does it mean to me?" or "How do I apply this?" I did my personal Bible study on that grid.

So, you took a few verses and paraphrased them in the left column to identify what the passage says. You identified main points and secondary points. That helped me. I could see an outline. Then I could explore what the passage meant using commentaries and other resources. Finally, I considered the third question, "What does it mean to me?" Those three simple things became the structure for how I started approaching life through the lens of Scripture.

My next step in ministry was learning to lead inductive Bible studies for small groups. I had to take what a passage says, what it means, and what it means to me and transform those ideas into related questions that allowed a small group to explore a Scripture in depth. "What does it say?" had to be transformed into observation questions. "What does it mean?" became interpretation questions. "What does it mean to me?" became application questions. I would actually write out questions that would give structure to a Bible study, and I'd write O beside observation portions, I beside interpretative questions, and A beside application questions.

I asked those questions to the group and logically led them through the discovery of the text. After a few years, however, we had a spiritual breakthrough and overnight, our group grew from a small discussion Bible study to sixty-five students, and then soon to a hundred people. With that size group, I couldn't ask questions and get feedback. I needed to structure whole messages. That happened during my second year of graduate school.

My students wanted to hear a sermon, to hear in-depth teaching. So I had to stand up and talk for half an hour. But simply sticking to observation, interpretation and application, and responding to the Holy Spirit's fire in our hearts, helped me to encourage them and call them to a deeper walk of faith.

When I married, my wife would say, "You need to tell more stories; you need to illustrate more." So I learned to combine the academic disciplines I had applied inductively to the wealth of stories in God's Word.

When I went to Southern California to pastor Newport-Mesa Christian Center following George O. Wood, the church was in phase one of a building program, so it took three services to get everyone in the building on Sunday morning. That experience of having to preach a message three times in a row helped me learn to be more economical with words—to really get to the core of a message.

I tell young pastors that if they have the opportunity to preach the same message multiple times, it helps them to develop as a preacher. During the first service, I'd usually find areas I needed to strengthen. Then, during second service, I could really tighten up the central message.

Somewhere along the line, I decided that I wanted to break out of the predictable three-point sermons. Some of my sermons have three points, but I wanted to break out of that predictableness. A very good preacher of a fairly contemporary church recently noted, "I found in my preaching that two points just wasn't quite enough, four points was too much, so I've settled again on the three-point sermon." But, in my case, I tried to make it a bit more unpredictable. I want to find the central thread of truth and then hear the applicational message from the Spirit of God. Then I put those things together. The structure doesn't always come out the same every week.

It is amazing how we are called to partner with the Scriptures in the act of teaching. We're handling the Word of God, which is one of the most important tasks anyone can ever undertake. It's more important than answering mail. It's more important than one-on-one counseling, more important than board meetings. It's more important than anything but our prayer life. And, I often mix my prayer life with sermon preparation.

When I do my personal Scripture reading, I read two chapters out of Old Testament history, three to five chapters out of Psalms, one chapter out of Proverbs, one chapter of the Gospels, one chapter out of Acts, and two chapters out of the Epistles. I try to do that at one sitting several times a week. It takes me about forty-five minutes.

I do that to keep a breadth of perspective on the whole amazing story of God's Word. And in the midst of it all, I always look for one verse that stands out to me from all the chapters I read. I'll go back and for another five minutes I will meditate on that one verse, saying it over again, reading it over and over. "God, get this into my heart," is my prayer. "Help me to get this. What are You trying to say to me?" That's where I cultivate a sense of listening to the voice of the Holy Spirit. Sometimes, I'll go back to a chapter and turn every verse into a prayer. That kind of life in the Word plus prayer is my baseline. That keeps me in touch with the whole story.

Message preparation requires priority time. Great preachers, effective people who really know how to feed their congregation, spend hours in a week looking at their text and praying about those to whom they are going to be ministering, listening to the Holy Spirit. We will explore all these things in this book. Sermon preparation takes time. If you are going to teach the Word, it must to be your number one priority as a spiritual leader. And it's going to require hard work and extended time. Sometimes it flows very easily in a particular week. But other times, I have to pace and pray in the Spirit and think about the text. And even then, I struggle to develop an outline.

At times, although rarely, I have used an outline someone else has preached simply because it is so well done. (But I've never taken a script from someone else and just read it.) I always give credit to that person up front. Once in a while, that person's outline captures the passages I'm studying; what I see in that outline really resonates in me and is a very close match to my own spiritual expression. But if you do that every week, it will show. People will get a sense that you are a bit artificial and your material is canned.

Preaching must be the expression of God's Word through you. I have to process Scripture through my own spirituality, in my own life, in my own mind. Then, I can simplify it. I can build the applications around the text, because I know the people to whom I am preaching, and I sense that I've heard from God for them.

Nothing compares to that sense of connecting with God, connecting with His Word, and connecting with His people.

2 Five Essential Premises for Effective Preaching

A popular speaker once quipped that he could prepare a sermon in two hours, but sometimes it took God two years to get him ready to preach it.

For all of us who preach, it is vitally important to answer the question, "Why am I preaching?" Some of us have an innate love of preaching. As I have said earlier, we can forget that people aren't there to give us a chance to preach. Rather, we're there to help people become. And what do they become? What is the standard toward which we are pointing them? What do we want them to become if they listen to us preach for five years? They should be different, better people than they are now.

The standard is Christlikeness. It's Jesus himself, and everything about His kingdom, His character, His understanding of the activity of the Holy Spirit, and His role as the Giver of the Spirit. Everything centers in Christlikeness.

God's Word preached must bring us to places of decision, confrontation and belief that affect what we become. As we considered in the last chapter, when we preach God's Word in light of 2 Timothy

3:16,17, it will be life changing. People are taught, rebuked, corrected and trained to prepare them for what Jesus purposes for them.

Preaching connects the information of the text with the transformation of people's lives. When I pray and prepare for a sermon, I sometimes think of information as, "Thus saith the text." We must work through the text to help people understand it in interesting and creative ways.

The transformation part is, "Thus saith the Lord." In addition to immersing myself in the text, I'll pace and pray. Sometimes I just pray in tongues. I'll say, "Lord, I know what the text says, but what specifically is consistent with the truth of this text that You want to say to people this week?" When people hear you preach with that perspective, they feel like they have been exposed to Scripture, but they have also heard a word from the Lord for them.

Another way of describing this process is the journey from belief to behavior. "Thus saith the text" tells us what to believe; "Thus saith the Lord" brings us to points of obedience in our behavior so transformation can happen. "Thus saith the text," the information side, is proclamation. We proclaim what God's Word says. Some of the preaching in our history was great proclamation. Our Movement was built by people who knew how to proclaim truth eloquently and powerfully. As the Word is proclaimed, there needs to be that prophetic sense on the part of the listener of, "Here's what God is nailing down in my own life through what I've heard." Good proclamational preaching needs to have that prophetic "Thus saith the Lord" overtone to it. That's why our prayer life is so important to the presentation.

Preaching is a journey from exposition to application. I find it helpful to think of preaching in terms of answering two questions, "What?" and "So what?" The "What?" addresses what the text says and what it means. The "So what?" relates to how the text affects our lives and what we should do in response to that truth.

We must constantly take into consideration the congregation's life circumstances. You may be preaching on Jesus feeding the five thousand, but someone out there may have a child who just ran away that week. Another person might be facing a job layoff. A sixty-seven-year-old woman in the congregation may have just received a very bad medical diagnosis that week. Those people might treat your message cynically—"Well, so what? Jesus fed five thousand people. How does that help my child, preserve my job, or address my illness?" I deeply believe the proclamational prophetic presentation of the content of God's Word can profoundly answer not only the "What?" but also the "So what?" questions. The transformation occurs where we bring the truth into direct contact with people's lives.

A popular speaker once quipped that he could prepare a sermon in two hours, but sometimes it took God two years to get him ready to preach it. His cleverness and penchant for overstatement amused me, but a question also began to dig away at me. Beyond good exegesis and skillful homiletics, what does it take on a personal level to speak the Word of God with authority and authenticity?

Ultimately, of course, we must come back to God's calling and qualifying us as His spokespersons. Unworthy and insufficient as we are to be His mouthpieces, it is still Christ's authority that commissions us, God's love that compels us, and the Holy Spirit who empowers us—especially in our weakness. However, the initiative of God to call and qualify us to preach does not make us passive participants when it comes to the preparation process. If Pentecost and exegesis are inseparable, so also are preparation and proclamation. The anointing of God's Spirit giving life to effective preaching and teaching is, in fact, the result of the preparation process—not a replacement for it. Furthermore, that preparation process is more than just a pen and paper exercise. It encompasses our whole life.

To explore the numerous dimensions of this "whole life" preparation, I will build on five assumptions, or premises. These premises will shape the structure for the rest of this chapter.

Premise 1: In the words of Jesus, "Apart from me you can do nothing" (John 15:5).

Jesus' teaching "Apart from me you can do nothing" left one spiritual leader asking herself: "What part of 'nothing' don't you understand?"[1] At issue is staying connected to the Divine Vine, Jesus Christ, in light of our inability to accomplish anything apart from the life flow of His Spirit. Yet, our tendency is to gravitate towards self-dependence. Preoccupation with what we bring to the preaching event blinds us to our utter barrenness apart from God's enablement. When this happens, our preaching becomes a tainted mixture of carnal flesh and holy fire. Arrogance, self-assured posturing, and image-centered performance will replace God's glory and the living fruit that only His Spirit can produce.

Paradoxically, when we are faithful to our part we can run the danger of eclipsing God's part. Stewardship of our giftings and a commitment to excellence rightfully require that we work as if a lot depended on us, but our heart must counterintuitively go in the other direction. "Apart from me you can do nothing," Jesus continues to remind us. How do we maintain such a poverty of spirit? The answer lies outside the boundaries of either productive study techniques or good personal life management. Coming to the end of ourselves is the fruit of only one thing—brokenness.

Given our natural aversion to such thinking, brokenness for most of us is not high on our list of "things most aspired to." But there is no replacement for it. "My sacrifice, O God, is a broken spirit; a broken and contrite heart you, God, will not despise" (Psalm 51:17).

When that humility and hunger genuinely converge in us, everything changes. "Grieve, mourn and wail. Change your laughter to mourning and your joy to gloom. Humble yourselves before the Lord, and he will lift you up" (James 4:9,10). Broken of self-sufficiency, self-dependence and self-promotion, we can finally move from a posture of working for Christ to one of Christ working through us. Referring to a list of spiritual giants such as D. L. Moody, Jonathan Goforth, George Müller, Hudson Taylor, Madam Guyon, Douglas Hyde, and Amy Carmichael, Miles Stanford estimates that it took, on average, "fifteen years after they entered their life work before they began to know the Lord Jesus as their life, and ceased trying to work for Him and began allowing Him to be their All in All and to do His work through them."[2] That remarkable transition takes testing. And it takes time. But, it radically transforms our ministry.

The apostle Paul spoke of brokenness and its fruit in the language of death and resurrection. "I want to know Christ—yes, to know the power of his resurrection and participation in his sufferings, becoming like him in his death, and so, somehow, attaining to the resurrection from the dead " (Philippians 3:10,11). We cannot have resurrection if we sidestep death. That is what the crucified life is all about. Jesus was likely crucified with three nails: We too need three death-dealing nails driven through the unbroken parts of our life—one through our rebellion, one through our reputation and one through our rights. This dying-to-self process gets us out of the way and opens our life to being truly and substantially filled with the Holy Spirit.

Where do spiritual disciplines fit into this process? In the words of Evan Howard, "Christian spiritual formation is not simply improving the regularity of prayer or Bible study. It is not merely becoming personally accountable for our sins. Christian spiritual formation is *the transformation of our spirit* through the Spirit of Christ."[3] Spiritual disciplines are a pathway to that end, they are not the end itself. Spiritual disciplines connect us to God and help us cultivate a hunger for God, in the sense that the more we pray, the more we usually want to pray. But by themselves, spiritual disciplines can be merely external religious activities if there is no brokenness that opens us to the Spirit's life. Howard explains it this way: "If we are not prepared to allow ourselves—mind, emotion, and will—to be *moved* by the Spirit, I doubt we will allow ourselves to be *formed* by the Spirit."[4]

Living out the reality that "apart from me you can do nothing" will in no way resemble the superficial spirituality all around us we are tempted to accept. As I have already pointed out, this requires more than merely having a daily quiet time, as important as that is, or properly preparing to preach a sermon for the next Sunday. Instead, this coming to the end of ourselves is a life of openness to the heart-deep dealings of the Lord who alone can reduce us and remake us.

And this is not a process that we can superintend. We can only invite it. Just as we cannot physically crucify ourself, brokenness and the crucified life are not our own doing but the action of God in us. Our part is to continually choose the posture of humility and hunger for God as we pursue a life of deepening faith and dependence. He alone knows how to truly discipline, purify, and break us. It is not necessary for us to embrace a sort of masochistic spirituality to help the process along. Rather, God himself is mercifully at work in us to increase our capacity to know and depend on Him. The end product will be much more than better sermons. It will be a joyful, Spirit-filled life.

Ray Beeson and Ranelda Mack Hunsicker describe one aspect of this breaking process in a vivid picture of purification:

> The Lord ... allows the heat to be turned up in life's pressure cooker. He carefully watches the gauge, knowing exactly how much we can bear. As the pot boils, some poisonous gases start to bubble up. Reeling from the foul odor that permeates our lives, we cry, 'Where did all this come from?' Sometimes we discover we've been building a temple to God

on a toxic waste dump of unresolved hurt. Then the Holy Spirit makes himself known to us as the refining fire rather than the gentle dove. He burns away the stench of rebellion, unforgiveness, pride—whatever is polluting our lives. He cauterizes the wound amid our screams. Finally he pours in the oil of healing and restores our joy.[5]

Premise 2: Ministry can be toxic to our spiritual health.

People who are not involved in preaching or vocational ministry have trouble understanding that ministry can be toxic to the minister's spiritual health. Nevertheless, the subtle and insidious dangers unique to ministry are lurking everywhere. Such dangers were evident in the religious world that Jesus walked into two thousand years ago. As James S. Stewart describes it, the Pharisees had "externalized" religion, the scribes had "professionalized" religion, the Sadducees had "secularized" religion, and the Zealots had "nationalized" religion.[6] Clearly, nothing has changed. Unless we are rigorous with our own heart, religious leadership will do the same to us—leaving us externalized, professionalized, incurably cynical, and far too political.

"Ministry" too easily becomes a surrogate for "spirituality." Norman Shawchuck and Roger Heuser explain it this way:

Many church leaders fall into the trap of equating ministry with spirituality. Ministry and spirituality are related, but they are not the same. Ministry consumes energy. Spirituality restores energy. Ministry not supported by an appropriate spirituality is ultimately doomed to boredom, stagnation, disappointment, infirmity.[7]

The consequences can be immense. They go on to point out:

The bad habits or temptations of the religious profession, when left unexamined, open the door to powerful, entrenched emotions, influencing the leader's subconscious to the effect that wrong looks right, or at least acceptable. Sooner or later an unexamined religious leadership will erode into neurotic dysfunctionality—which both the leader and the congregation exhibit.[8]

Christian psychologist Richard D. Dobbins diagnoses the problem in terms of a tension in vocational ministry between "walk" and "work":

There is no necessary correlation between a minister's walk with God and his work for God. His ministerial work may be statistically successful, but that doesn't mean his relationship with God is healthy. It simply means he is talented and skilled in the work he does; he is good at the work of the ministry. However, the minister can be a personal failure at the same time he is a professional success. The shock of such a discovery is a blessing in disguise when it forces the minister to focus more on his walk than his work. Nothing pleases the Lord more, *for He is much more interested in our walk than He is in our work.*[9]

At a crucial time in my own development as a young, single pastor, I came to understand that partnership with God in vocational ministry is like being married with children. It is not uncommon to see couples divorce after twenty-five or thirty years of marriage, once the children have left home. Left to themselves, the husband and the wife realize for the first time that they are strangers. For years everything in their marriage revolved around the children. This bred partnership but not relationship.

The crisis that brought this realization in my own life came at a time when I was pastoring a successful, growing church and even praying one or two hours a day. But everything in my spirituality revolved around the congregation, my "spiritual children." The intimacy of knowing and walking with Jesus simply for who Jesus is had eluded me. Joy had gone from my life, a fact many people noticed, and my preaching took to pushing people more than nourishing them. I grew increasingly cynical and impatient with everything ministry related.

The prescription for me was to spend every Saturday night for six months alone with God in my room. Praying for ministry concerns or even the message the next day felt off-limits. Instead, I would strum my guitar and sing worship songs to the Lord. Or I would lie on my face on the carpet and groan in prayer, agonizing over what was missing in my life. At other times, I would sit cross-legged on my bed with my eyes wide open and just tell Jesus all the reasons why I loved Him.

Nothing happened immediately, but over time my joy began to return. I also began to experience God's presence in extraordinary ways. It became clear to me that we serve and we preach out of a spiritual life that is separate from serving and preaching. Otherwise we are neither authentic nor lastingly fruitful. It also became abundantly clear to me that ministry can become idolatry if it is not founded on intimacy with God. At this point vocational ministry, the preaching ministry in particular, becomes extremely toxic spiritually.

The antidote to such a toxic life is a secret life with God. It starts with regularly devouring quantities of Scripture that have nothing to do with what we are going to preach on. We need not only to read the Scriptures, but let the Scriptures "read" to us; that is, make ourselves the first responder when it comes to obeying what we read. We also need to pray the Scriptures back to God, letting them become the heart language of our own yearnings for Him. How tragic if we would value God's Word only for the material it provides us for preaching!

If we are to avoid the toxicity of public ministry, we must also become authentic worshippers. This is more than just leading in worship. It is a life centered in the kind of Christ-directed adoration that keeps one's focus on Him, not just on His children. A worshipful lifestyle will even affect our response to corporate worship before we preach. Rather than using that time to go over our message once more, we find ourselves wanting to engage God's presence personally as a worshipper. In spite of needing to be aware of what is going on in the service, we cannot help but be preoccupied with God himself.

Praying extensively in tongues during those secret times with God also keeps our heart nourished, dependent and spiritually alive (1 Corinthians 14:4,14). The very act of praying out loud, in fact, conditions our mouths to give expression to the urging and utterances of the Spirit within us. Praying alone out loud is great training for preaching. But more importantly, praying in tongues connects our spirituality to the passions of God's heart in a healthy way. When our heart and God's heart are in sync, then ministry no longer substitutes for spirituality but is a genuine expression of it.

We need to do whatever it takes to regularly renew our spiritual vitality, to stay spiritually alive and authentic. Underlying everything should be a renunciation of all ambitions other than knowing and pleasing God.

A.W. Tozer captured this best in a prayer he wrote on the night of his ordination into ministry:

Lord Jesus, I come to Thee for spiritual preparation. Lay Thy hand upon me. Anoint me with the oil of the New Testament prophet. Forbid that I should become a religious scribe and thus lose my prophetic calling. Save me from the curse that lies dark across the modern clergy, the curse of compromise, of imitation, of professionalism. Save me from the error of judging a church by its size, its popularity or the amount of its yearly offering. Help me to remember that I am a prophet—not a promoter, not a religious manager, but a prophet. Let me never become a slave to crowds. Heal my soul of carnal ambitions and deliver me from the itch for publicity.... I am Thy servant to do Thy will, and that will is sweeter to me than position or riches or fame and I choose it above all things on earth or in heaven.[10]

Premise 3: There must be alignment between God's Word as the message and our life as the messenger.

Paul is unequivocal with Timothy about the alignment of message and messenger: "Watch your *life* and *doctrine* closely. Persevere in them, because if you do, you will save both yourself and your hearers" (1 Timothy 4:16, my emphasis). "Life" and "doctrine," messenger and message—there is to be no disconnect or misalignment between them. In fact, according to Paul, the degree to which we "persevere" in the study of scriptural truth (doctrine) in preparation for preaching is the same degree to which we should persevere in paying attention to the consistency of our own life.

When it comes to preaching, I would not ascribe completely to Marshall McLuhan's popular assertion that "the medium is the message." God's Word stands with potency and authority independent of our inadequate lives as communicators of it. Yet we must never forget that we exegete the text of Scripture in part by the way we live the text ourselves. We preach as much by lifestyle as by proclamation. In the words of Mother Teresa: "Just allow people to see Jesus in you; to see how you pray, to see how you lead a pure life, to see how you deal with your family, to see how much peace there is in your family. Then you can look straight into their eyes and say, 'This is the way.' You speak from life, you speak by experience."[11]

Anecdotally, we all know that our actions usually do speak louder than our words. Being a spiritual leader means that we first make a commitment to be obedient followers of Christ ourself. Then, when we preach, we are merely inviting others to change and grow with us as we follow Christ (1 Corinthians 11:1). This is preaching that is not only text centered but also life applicational. It engenders in us a personal transparency that listeners respond to in surprisingly significant ways.

In wrestling with Paul's call for Timothy to pay close attention to both his life and his doctrine as a preacher, I have formulated seven two-word imperatives to characterize the life of the messenger behind the message. With each of these imperatives comes a diagnostic question.

1. KNOW GOD: If the preaching ministry were taken from me, would I still have a personal, growing relationship with Jesus?

2. PURSUE INTEGRITY: Are there areas of ongoing secrecy in my life I am trying to hide from those closest to me?

3. BE YOURSELF: How often do I hear people say, "Pastor, thank you for your authenticity"?

4. OWN RESPONSIBILITY: Do I acknowledge my mistakes, or do I project blame and use the pulpit to vent unresolved anger?

5. EMBRACE CHANGE: Is my attitude faith filled and future focused, or am I overly nostalgic about the past and fearful of taking risks in the present?

6. LOVE LEARNING: Am I coasting intellectually, or am I applying myself to the disciplines of personal study and reflection?

7. LIVE JOYFULLY: Am I living under the self-imposed pressure of always having to prove something to somebody?

Michael Cavanagh uses the analogy of a violin to describe the need for attentiveness to our personal life:

A violin is a musical instrument that is both sensitive and strong. It is sensitive in that it is affected by the slightest touch, and it is strong because its strings can withstand a good deal of pressure. A violin must be continually and properly tuned to be played well, for if it is not, even the finest violinist cannot call forth beautiful music from it. . . . When ministers are in tune with themselves, they can touch people in beautiful ways, but when they are out of tune with themselves, not even the Lord can make music with them.[12]

King David modeled for us a very courageous prayer: "Search me, God, and know my heart" (Psalm 139:23). Rigorous honesty with ourselves must be the relentless pursuit of our lives as preachers and teachers. That pursuit, of course, is fraught with fears and diversions; otherwise, we would all do it easily and well. Defensiveness, rationalization, people pleasing, externalism, busyness, fatigue— they all serve to sidestep authentic honesty with ourself and deceive us into settling for image over integrity. We fall into the trap of exegeting Scripture for its truth while not truthfully exegeting our own heart. The resulting disconnect between message and messenger can be masked for a while, but it will eventually manifest itself in shallowness and internal hollowness. Compartmentalizing our life and refusing to deal with the painful parts will be spiritually deadly.

Ultimately, the journey towards internal honesty leads us to the conclusion that our biggest problem is our own heart. We are tempted to think our biggest problem as preachers is overcoming sermon block, facing financial challenges, or negotiating with parishioners who can seriously complicate our life on any given day. That is not the case. (Some of them are beyond our control anyhow.) Our greatest challenge and hardest work is taking responsibility for the attitudes and health of our own heart, in spite of what is going on around us. Internal victories must walk hand in hand with external victories; otherwise, something of true stamina and authenticity is lost over the long run.

Taking responsibility for our own heart while trying to lead others spiritually will usually require the presence of both people and the Holy Spirit in our life. Trusted people who know us well can help us to be honest with ourself when we lack the courage and want to duck the issues. Usually, we will need to give permission to such people to address us in this way. But if we are to regularly address others with the counsels of God, being so addressed ourself is not optional. To ensure the health of our own heart and the integrity of our lifestyle, we need to make sure there are people in our life who know us well, see us often, and talk with us honestly.

This involves a determination on our part to talk about what is really going on inside us, and then listen for feedback. If we are married, this begins with our spouse. They often read us more accurately than we read ourself. Their persistent concerns, and even warnings, should not go unheeded through overreaction, hypersensitivity or denial. On at least a monthly basis, a small group of accountability partners should have the privilege of asking us the hard questions—not only concerning our vulnerability to particular sins, but concerning our attitudes, motivations and strategies for health. Spiritual health starts with honesty, and that honesty is usually too difficult for any of us to navigate alone.

Besides giving us people for our life, God gives us the gift of His own Spirit. "Lord, fill me with Your Spirit" is one of the most important prayers we can pray. The humility and hunger that flow out of brokenness will bring us back to this cry again and again. Being attentive to our intimacy with Jesus, beyond mere activity for Him, will constantly deepen our passion for His Spirit in our life. And our desire for both "life" and "doctrine" to line up will necessitate the Spirit's work in us in very holistic ways. Being Pentecostal means more than being anointed when we preach; it means being full of the Holy Spirit whether we preach or not.

Stanley M. Horton observes,

> When the Sadducees questioned Jesus about the resurrection He told them, "You are in error because you do not know the Scriptures or the power of God" (Matthew 22:29). My thesis is that you cannot truly know the Scriptures apart from the power of God. Knowing only the letter kills "but the Spirit gives life" (2 Corinthians 3:6).[13]

Horton goes on to describe the pathway to that power in terms of repentance.

> Let us believe and claim Acts 3:19 where the Greek indicates we can have times of refreshing from the Lord until Jesus comes again. But they only come when there is genuine repentance.... Where do I need to repent? Where do you?[14]

Repentance realigns everything in our life with Christ's lordship and our preaching. It is the direct doorway to Spirit fullness once we have been honest with God under the conviction of His Spirit.

Premise 4: Time is the most valuable commodity we have and needs to be managed.

I have a friend who has consulted professionally with executives in the oil industry. One day we were discussing what distinguished exceptional CEOs from good ones. His answer, from working closely with many of them, had nothing to do with differing skill levels. Instead, the exceptional leaders had developed an intuitive gift, which others had not, for knowing the most important things to do on any given day, and then doing them. As another friend of mine put it, "I am not necessarily smarter than anyone else—I am just better organized. That way I am always a step ahead of the crowd."

Just like money, time needs to be managed well if we are to leverage its potential. We do that by prioritizing and planning in advance rather than on the run. Priorities must ultimately be reduced to those very few most important things that need to be done in a week to fulfill one's core mission. For those who preach, adequate study, prayer and reflection time need to be at the top of that short list.

The next challenge for most of us is follow-through. It is generally easier to do what we feel like doing or what brings us the most immediate gratification rather than doing what we planned ahead to do. However, the most common decisions we face as church leaders are generally not choices between good and evil, but between good and most important. Of the many ways we could use two hours in a given day, what is the best thing we could do in light of our priorities? Urgencies and expectations too often cause us to sacrifice the spiritual preparation and study time essential to effective and anointed preaching. In those famous words of Goethe: "Things which matter most must never be at the mercy of things which matter least."

Many pastors with preaching responsibilities find it helpful to plan their weeks in half-day blocks of time, and then primarily do only one type of work in each of those blocks, such as counseling, administration, visitation, leadership development, and, of course, study. Usually half-day blocks are sufficient periods to accommodate interruptions and still engage a task adequately. Doing many different things in a short period of time may be exhilarating, but it usually also keeps us from engaging important things sufficiently. Message preparation, in particular, requires an extended focus. Additionally, it deserves those blocks of hours in a day when we are the most intuitive and creative. Some of us are much more creative in the morning hours, others, at night. To be honest, some of us are also most creative when we are pressed by deadlines and feel the adrenaline-pumping pressure to produce. This is all right as long as the more compressed blocks still allow time for thorough preparation of their tasks. Time of week as well as time of day are important. Deadline pressure is not an excuse to procrastinate until Saturday night. Rather, it is a dynamic that can pace the preparation of a message throughout the week in a way that meshes best with how we are individually wired to work.

The creative process is a fascinating one, unique to each of us. Few universal rules exist. In general, however, creativity requires two things, *concentration* and *context*. Concentration functions in uncluttered, open spaces of time: time to pray and let a message gestate in our spirit, time to dream new thoughts and let God speak to us, time to distance ourself mentally from those tasks that interrupt and dampen our creativity. We are generally most creative when we have extended blocks of time just to dream, pray, and think without pressures or distractions. I call it "psychological space." In corporate leadership literature, it is often referred to as "staring out the window time." Most of us do far too little of it, and to that degree, our creativity is diminished.

In addition to concentration, creativity requires context. Context refers to the "where" of the creative process. What settings trigger the creative juices in you? Where are you most reflective and prayerful? Where are your study tools most accessible to you? Does walking enhance your ability to think clearly or pray intentionally? Are there specific locations where God regularly seems to meet with you? What stimulates your imagination and puts you in a creative mind-set? Do certain types of music put you in an intuitive mood? These are questions that no one can answer for you because creative context is so individual to each one of us. However, many pastors have a study place that is separate from the church office in order to physically, and therefore psychologically, segment administrative work from intuitive work.

Beyond seizing on creative times of the day or week, time management needs to assume a yearly rhythm as well. Spontaneity from week to week may get us by for a while, but in order to offer a balanced spiritual diet in our preaching, we need to see the big picture. To lay out a preaching plan for the entire year, take advantage of the larger blocks of time that may be found in the summer months. The rest of the year can be interspersed with study and prayer days out of the office. Planning ahead by booking those days before other things book them up for us is obviously the key. No one can do that for us. That is why we call it *time management*.

In his book on pastoring "turnaround churches," Gene Wood includes a helpful appendix with fifty time-management suggestions.

Here are a few of them:

1. Just say NO.
2. Hold stand-up meetings. People will stick with the focus of the meeting if not allowed to sit.
3. Use a time-analysis sheet for a week. Compare (in 15-minute blocks) what you planned to do versus what you actually did. Are there patterns?
4. Habitually carry 3 x 5 cards or self-adhesive notes.
5. Do mundane but necessary tasks in your down time.
6. Handle (most) paper only once! (We usually don't do this because we are afraid to make decisions.)
7. Develop a habit of punctuality.
8. Avoid events and invitations that serve only to boost your ego.
9. Become a filer, not a piler.
10. When possible, do first what you dislike doing.
11. Scrutinize ongoing commitments harder than onetime commitments.
12. Delegate low priority items that won't have much impact to someone who can do them 80 percent as well as you can.[15]

Premise 5: For great preaching to occur, our heart must converge with our head.

I like to put it this way: When we preach we want both our head and our heart to come out of our mouth. The head represents an understanding of the truth of the text and the heart represents the spirit in which we minister that text. Jesus said that true worship is integrative, involving both "spirit" and "truth" (John 4:24). The merging of head and heart is therefore the merging of mind and spirit, content and conviction, principles and passion, intellect and inspiration, exposition and empathy, ethos and pathos. It is the fusion of "Thus saith the text" with "Thus saith the Lord."

Using a different word picture to say the same thing, Edgar R. Lee writes:

> Intellectual and spiritual growth must proceed on parallel tracks joined like a railroad with innumerable cross ties, thus comprising one avenue to meaningful life and service. Intellectual growth alone leads to rationalism; spiritual intensity alone to fanaticism. It is clear that our Lord never intended a bifurcation between mind and spirit—a stereotype allowed too long to flourish in our church.[16]

The preparation of our heart for effective preaching has been the subject of the first three premises of this chapter. A brokenness before God, a commitment to intimacy with Christ before activity for Christ, and a determination to line up our life with our message—all play a role in shaping our heart with the purity and passion that great preaching requires. The role of our mind, however, is too often overlooked. Some default to the old adage, "When the point is weak, just shout louder." The problem is that some tend to do nothing but shout.

Disciplined thoughtfulness and deep theological reflection, however, have always been essential building blocks of Pentecostal faith and proclamation. Gary B. McGee reminds us: "Contrary to the criticisms of opponents, Pentecostals come from a rich background of doctrinal and biblical reflection."[17] William and Robert Menzies observe, "It is significant that the Pentecostal revival began among Christian believers who were studying the Bible. A hunger for truth, not merely a quest for experience, energized these early seekers."[18]

The Latin word for "priest" in *pontifex*, which appropriately derives from the Latin words for "bridge builder." In preaching, we certainly build bridges between the "there and then" and the "here and now." But we also build another kind of bridge—the bridge between God and humanity. The priest represented God to the people and the people to God. Whenever we preach, we do the same, for it is at the crossroads of the Scriptures that God's sovereignty intersects with humanity's situation. It is therefore incumbent upon us as effective "priestly" preachers to learn all we can about God and all we can about people. We must become thoroughly acquainted with both the throne room of God and the marketplace of humanity.

We learn by reading, listening, observing and experiencing. Opportunities for continuing education abound, both formally and informally. A commitment to be a lifelong learner is a commitment to defy intellectual laziness and the kind of careless message preparation that brings into it little true understanding of either God or people. It is a commitment to time alone with God, disciplined study of Scripture, and time with people. Although I pastored churches large enough to consume all my time in administration, problem solving, and preaching, I always found it important to continue connecting with new ideas as well as leaving time in my schedule for doing some pastoral counseling. Stretching intellectually through study and listening carefully to people's struggles through one-on-one interactions are simple but potent ways of learning that tangibly improve preaching.

Concerning our reading, Shawchuck and Heuser suggest:

> One must learn to read according to one's fundamental priorities and learning needs. Find the books that are written by those who are masters at the craft and devour them. Further, when you find a book that speaks to you in an out-of-the-ordinary way, devour everything the author has written. Allow the author to become your companion-in-absentia. Twenty books read at random will do less good for keeping one's brain awake, and hatching new ideas, than will the thorough digestion of five books written by the masters in one's learning area.[19]

For other kinds of general reading, get the gist of the book without reading it word for word. The famous 80-20 rule can be applied: 20 percent of the book usually contains 80 percent of the content. Read the table of contents and the first and last chapters first. Then scan quickly the rest of the chapters looking for the key thesis of each chapter (sometimes found in the first and last paragraphs of each chapter or in sectional headings). Of course, books with summaries at the end of each chapter simplify such work for us.

Learning all we can about God and His truth, as well as learning all we can about people and their needs, deepens the substance of our messages and broadens our capacity to apply Scripture meaningfully to people's lives. More important than saying something loudly is saying something meaningfully. People are fed spiritually when we have done our homework. Thinking deeply about scriptural truth and thinking attentively about the issues people face and then bringing the two together lays the groundwork for content-filled preaching. Having something to say that is both revelational and relevant, structured in a way people can follow, is the fruit of both head and heart coming out of the mouth.

This takes more than inspiration. It takes hard work. Pastor Bill Wilson, Oregon district superintendent who pastored Portland Metro Assembly of God in Portland, Oregon, gives us some practical suggestions for getting started.

1. Stake out your own pastor's study.
2. Draw up a consistent schedule of weekly preparation.
3. Organize the room to be efficient and inviting.
4. Prepare a workable filing system according to subject.
5. Form a plan to add quality and helpful resources regularly.
6. Inform the church of the one day a week given to study.
7. Expect tremendous times of reward and revelation.[20]

Finally, in addition to learning all you can about God's truth and people's needs, make it your goal to learn how to become a great communicator. Read books on preaching and public speaking. Listen to yourself on tape, as painful as that usually is. Then listen to people who are truly great communicators and ask yourself some questions: What do they do to truly engage and keep the audience's attention? How do they integrate head and heart issues to make messages truly meaningful? Where does the message start, where does it end, and how do they keep things on track? How are their introductions and conclusions structured? How is their communication style consistent both with who they are (authenticity) and what they are trying to say (content)? How do they paint word pictures or use humor effectively? Which points do they choose to illustrate and how?

The next step is to get structured feedback from others on your own preaching. As I described in the last chapter, I once felt I had plateaued as a preacher and was struggling to get to the next level on my own. After consulting with one of my associate pastors, I formed a sermon committee (for lack of a better term)—a cross-section of the people who listened to me preach week after week.

The people in the group were amazingly helpful when it came to the practicality, organization and communication of my messages. I also appreciated their coaching me as a communicator without forcing me to be someone I was not. Each of us will be unique in our preaching style and approach to Scripture. In the words of George O. Wood,

The best definition of preaching I ever heard was "Preaching is you." It's the divine communication of truth through your human personality. None of us will preach exactly the same way from any given text, but those who preach the Word

will find the Lord at work in their own life and the lives of
the people they pastor.[21]

Preaching well is worth the best of our efforts. Preparing both
our heart and our mind thoroughly and then bringing them together
in the proclamation of God's timeless truth is the key. This kind of
whole-life preparation calls us first of all to a life of brokenness, dying
to any vestiges of self-sufficiency or self-promotion. Second, it warns
of the toxic effects of mistaking spirituality for ministry; we must
commit ourself to a lifestyle of intimacy with Christ whether or not
we are preaching. Third, the pathway to effective preaching challenges
us to bring into alignment what we preach with how we live. The
disconnect between message and messenger must go. Fourth, with
those inner victories of the heart won, we manage our time in ways
that cultivate creativity and carve out sufficient space in our schedule
for thorough study and reflection. Finally, being prepared to preach
sets us on a course of lifelong learning as we develop not only
spiritually, but intellectually. Our ambition becomes that of learning
all we can about God and all we can about people, and bringing them
together under the anointing of the Holy Spirit when we preach.

The ability to preach well is worth the hard work and life discipline that it requires. May we all respond to God's call on our lives to
be preachers that are fully prepared. Indeed, may we again hear and
obey the charge of Scripture itself: "Do your best to present yourself
to God as one approved, a workman who does not need to be ashamed
and who correctly handles the word of truth" (2 Timothy 2:15).

[1] Mindy Caliguire, "Soul Health," *Leadership* (Summer 2004): 42.

[2] Miles Stanford, *Principles of Spiritual Growth* (Grand Rapids, MI: Zondervan, 1975), 7,8.

[3] Evan Howard, "Three Temptations of Spiritual Formation," *Christianity Today* (December 9, 2002): 48; Howard's emphasis.

[4] Ibid., 49; Howard's emphasis.

[5] Ray Beeson and Ranalda Mack Hunsicker, *The Hidden Price of Greatness* (Wheaton, IL: Tyndale House, 1991), 176.

[6] James S. Stewart, *The Life and Teaching of Jesus Christ* (Nashville, TN: Abingdon Press, 1984), 24.

[7] Norman Shawchuck and Roger Heuser, *Leading the Congregation* (Nashville, TN: Abingdon Press, 1993), 120.

[8] Ibid., 96.

[9] Richard D. Dobbins, "Staying Healthy in the Ministry," in *The Pentecostal Pastor*, ed. Thomas E. Trask, Wayde I. Goodall, and Zenas J. Bicket (Springfield, MO: Gospel Publishing House, 1997), 146; Dobbins's emphasis.

[10] A.W. Tozer, "The Prayer of a Minor Prophet," http://articles.ochristian.com/article135.shtml (accessed May 15, 2001).

[11] Mother Teresa, *Words to Love By* (Notre Dame IN: Ave Maria Press, 1983), 15.

[12] Michael E. Cavanagh, *The Effective Minister* (San Francisco: Harper and Row, 1986), 1.

[13] Stanley M. Horton, *Reflections of an Early American Pentecostal* (Baguio City, Philippines: APTS Press, 2001), 1.

[14] Ibid., 102.

[15] Gene Wood, *Leading Turnaround Churches* (Carol Stream, IL: ChurchSmart Resources, 2001), 164–167.

[16] Edgar R. Lee, "Parameters for Seminary Education," *Assemblies of God Educator* (January-March 1989): 4,5.

[17] Gary B. McGee, *People of the Spirit* (Springfield, MO: Gospel Publishing House, 2004), 85.

[18] William W. Menzies and Robert P. Menzies, *Spirit and Power* (Grand Rapids, MI: Zondervan, 2000), 25.

[19] Shawchuck and Heuser, *Leading the Congregation*, 89.

[20] Bill Wilson, "The Pastor's Study," in *Pentecostal Pastor*, 78,79.

[21] George O. Wood, "Expository Preaching," in *Pentecostal Pastor*, 82.

3 One Message, One Truth

Every message you preach must communicate the unvarnished truth of God's Word, and with rare exceptions that will demand of you a personal, prayerful focus on one key idea.

Few verses of Scripture are more inspiring than Philippians 4:13. Many of us grew up with the King James Version rendering, "I can do all things through Christ which strengtheneth me." Just imagine the possibilities for our life if we truly took that verse to heart. Nothing would be beyond our grasp.

At least that is what you might think from the majority of sermons with that verse as their central text. "Look out, world! Here comes a truly empowered follower of Christ to proclaim God's truth and right all wrongs!" Throw in a prosperity spin, as many on-air preachers do, and you have a recipe for a full bank account, a spacious home, and late-model luxury cars.

By that point, the apostle Paul's intended message has been completely obliterated. Jump back to verse 11 and you can rediscover Paul's focus. I would paraphrase the apostle's remarks this way: "I've learned to be content in all things. I do well when I have a lot. I've also learned to do well without, because somehow my state of life internally is detached from my external circumstances." Then he ends by saying, "I can do all things through Christ who strengthens me."

I've asked groups, "What would you say is the main theme that ties that whole paragraph together in just one word or phrase?" Usually the first thing they will say, in light of verse 13, is: "The main theme is that we can do anything through Christ. We're overcomers. We're victorious." Yet, that idea does not tie together all the verses. Yes, it is true that Christ can empower us to do anything, but that is only part of the meaning intended by just the last sentence in that paragraph.

What ties all the sentences together? It's one word, contentment. I'm amazed how long it takes people to come to that answer because of their tunnel vision on the punch at the ending. Paul was asking, "How can I live detached from the world around me?" His answer: "In Christ, I can do all things. Humanly, that's a pretty tough thing to do. But in Christ, I can do all things."

To be fair to the text and to truly communicate its meaning, you need to understand Paul's original intention was to talk about the importance of contentment and how Christ's overcoming power actually can help us live out that godly characteristic. I *can* do all things through Christ, but the issue is being content.

Every message you preach must communicate the unvarnished truth of God's Word, and with rare exceptions that will demand of you a personal, prayerful focus on one key idea. As you identify and clearly present the foundational truth of your chosen text, you will create the best possible environment to accomplish preaching's primary goal—life change.

Purpose and Response

The basic structure of a message begins with identifying the central purpose of that message. That central purpose, of course, is related to the text of Scripture you are using. When you are studying a paragraph or a couple of paragraphs out of the text, you begin by looking for the one common word or phrase that ties everything in those paragraphs together. If you don't do this task well up front, you'll end up trying to say too many things as you develop your outline.

When you present a topical message, it is obviously easier to identify that one concept. If I'm going to talk about how to share Christ with my neighbor, for example, I will try to pull together verses from throughout Scripture based on the purpose I've already decided on ahead of time. But here again, you need to discipline yourself in establishing a succinct topic. The purpose for your message really needs to be short enough that you can say it, ideally, in a phrase or sentence. You want to avoid auxiliary issues. Ask yourself, "What is my central purpose? I am preaching this sermon about . . ." and you fill in the blank.

In one particular book on biblical preaching, the author talks about the subject and the complement. That's a little more of a sophisticated way of describing this process. You identify your subject: "What am I talking about?" Then you compose the complement: "What am I saying about the subject I'm talking about?"

My message preparation focuses strongly on the text. I never underestimate the vital importance of that component of my preparation. This goes beyond simply reading a passage of Scripture. It is finding the central thread of truth that ties the passage together and then deciding on the purpose of the message as it relates to people's lives. Since the underlying purpose of every message is life change, then I want to nurture a sense of connection between the text and the people.

Scripture is so rich in meaning. My goal is to discern what the Lord would say through me in this message out of the various possible applications of the text. I want to reach the point after prayer and meditation where I can say with a deep sense of conviction, "This is the purpose of *this* message." That epiphany on my part must be equally clear to those hearing the Word. When people walk out of the sanctuary after my time behind the pulpit, they need to be able to say, "He was talking about Subject A." Just as important, or even more important, they need to follow up that concept with, "I need to take Action B in response to Subject A."

Even a focused message may allow you to say several things about that one thing. There may be several applications to implement that one truth in life, but basically you're talking about only one thing.

Unless you clearly identify the one connecting thread within those verses and how that idea fits into the logic of the chapter's flow, you can literally preach five unrelated messages in one sermon. And when you have too many subjects in the message, you tend not to do application very well.

I believe it is far better to proclaim: "Here is the central idea; here is what God is saying to us today out of this text. Here is what this text says at its most fundamental level." Then you have time to work application into the very fabric of a life encounter by clearly sharing that one purpose in that passage of Scripture.

Determining the purpose of your message is like a two-sided coin. On one side, you are identifying that central concept, or the "What?," that ties all the verses in your message together. On the other side of the purpose statement "coin" is your message's "So what?" component. You want your congregation to ask themselves, "So what do I do with the truth I've just heard?" Purpose really answers two questions. What is the central thread, or central message, that unites all the verses? Then, what is the objective for people to live out when they walk away from this message?

Sometimes communicators commit the cardinal sin of random rhetoric. You can't follow what they are trying to say. They talk about this and they talk about that, and there's no straight line between "what" and "so what." Sometimes a secondary issue in the text will drag the unfocused preacher down a rabbit trail that dilutes the message and fogs over the desired application. The speaker just wanders all over the place, and if you were to interview members of the congregation you would find their plans of action in response to the message were equally diluted and foggy.

If you want to go from Chicago to New York City, you can get on Interstate 80 and drive there directly. You can fly nonstop from O'Hare to LaGuardia. But imagine how long the journey would be if you followed side roads to Texas, or Louisiana, and back up. Imagine deliberately scheduling a flight through three intermediate airports. Such a journey would only frustrate you. You can't go from start to finish in the most direct line and at the same time follow every detour. And when you are effectively communicating God's Word, you can't clearly present a central purpose and call to action while at the same time outlining every unrelated idea you encountered in your message preparation.

Simplicity does not mean simplistic. There comes a profoundness to the truly focused message. When you have done the hard work to think through a passage to the heart of its truth and have clearly identified the actions people should take as a result, your message will be less complicated but more profound. You will have a greater impact.

Starting Strong

Some speakers spend a lot of time on the titles they give to their messages. I can see the value of an aptly titled sermon, but I think one needs to exercise caution so that the title doesn't sink to the level of a pun or promise more than the message can deliver.

I used to come up with creative but rather obscure message titles. My goal was to pique the interest of the community and draw people into the church. In such cases, the title is designed to pique people's curiosity, often by raising questions in their mind.

For instance, you might come up with a title such as, "The Five Things God Can't Do." For example, God can't *not* love you. I suspect a careful examination of Scripture would turn up at least five things

God can't do because they violate His nature. That is the kind of message title you might find useful if you are advertising a special outreach or you want to grab people's attention. Their curiosity will shift into gear. You'll have them wondering, "Huh, five things God *can't* do? What could God not do?"

More and more, however, I forego the fancy title in favor of clearly identifying the central purpose of my message. For week-by-week pastoral preaching, I've discovered that attention-getting titles don't accomplish as much as a clear title of purpose. Titles can be overrated. It is always the substance of a message with the impact of the Holy Spirit that matters.

Contemporary audiences increasingly want to know why you are going to take up the next thirty minutes of their time, especially if they are unbelievers. People look for authenticity, and if you throw out a title with more hype than heft, you may get their attention at the expense of accomplishing the Holy Spirit's purpose for that moment.

Starting strong in your message also calls for a thought-provoking introduction. I try to tell people up front why they should hear me. But that calls for more than a bland statement. "Okay, we're talking about this, and here's why you need to listen." You've already shot down the greater portion of your audience's receptivity.

A powerful story provides a solid foundation for everything else you want to say. At the heart of that story must be the seed of your central purpose for that message. Within those first minutes of emotionally evocative narrative, your listeners needs to be able to identify the central idea you are trying to communicate and how you want them to respond. The story illustrates truth and opens up the kind of questions they need to be asking themselves and therefore why they need to hear what the biblical text is saying.

A good story introduces the subject or touches a felt need for which people want an answer. "Well, that brings up an issue. That raises a question. I can relate to that." A story garners their attention and helps keep them with you, ready to continue listening to what you want to say. It's much less intimidating for individuals to find common ground with you through a story than to be confronted with a list of truths you want to present.

Invitation to a Journey

Let's consider the fundamental issue of how you know what to preach on. What Scriptures do you use? What theme do you identify?

When I was pastoring, I took a different approach depending on the service. On Wednesday night, we usually held a Bible study and prayer meeting. I would teach verse by verse through a book of the Bible. In my understanding of the pastor's mandate, he or she carries the responsibility to regularly feed the flock the Word of God. I felt like pure Bible study was something I needed to be doing with my congregation.

The key sermon for me is Sunday morning. That's when I have the largest crowd. That's also when I have the most diverse group of people, according to age and spiritual maturity. You've got unbelievers there and seasoned saints. For Sunday morning preaching, I would include more application and always factor in the unbelievers who might attend that meeting. Unbelievers tend to accept invitations to church more on Sunday morning than Sunday night.

With our regular church attendees coming on Sunday nights, I would present deeper life issues, talking about walking in the Spirit or healing, and then taking time to pray with or wait on God with them. It gave me an opportunity to visit the kinds of Scripture texts that would help people open up to encounters with the power of God.

Some pastors will spend practically years going verse by verse through a book of the Bible in a Sunday service. I don't trust my abilities enough to keep people's attention that long. On Sunday mornings, I would usually do two to three series out of a book of the Bible in a given year. I generally also do two shorter topical series for perhaps five to seven weeks each. I might offer a couple of even shorter series that are also topical—two or three weeks on stewardship each year, and perhaps a four-week series on marriage or family.

Even when I'm preaching topically, I try to find one text a week for Sunday morning and generally stick to that. I may bring other supporting verses from other places, but primarily I'll take one text and say, "This is what this passage of Scripture says to us." Even topically, it is important to stay with a central idea from the text.

Each year includes a number of "stand-alones," such as Easter Sunday, Mother's Day and Christmas. These services offer unique opportunities to speak the truth into the lives of visitors who may not come any other time of year. Sometimes Mother's and Father's Days are ignored, but they can be great outreach days to visiting family members.

A theme during the year can also help your congregation maintain a spiritual focus. When I was pastoring Central Assembly in Springfield, Missouri, I put a theme to every year. One was "Year of the Spirit." One was "Year of Missions." One was "Year of the Volunteer." I like an annual emphasis for several reasons. It gives a point of unity and focus for the next stage developmentally that everybody throughout the life of the church can use. It can even guide a church in budget formation. But an annual theme is far more than just a good organizational idea. I really felt like our church's themes were something the Spirit of God gave to us. And His leading is paramount.

Listening to the Spirit

The people are not there to give me a chance to use my preaching gift. Neither am I preaching to get through another Sunday and keep my job. Bottom line, God wants to and must speak to people. Every week God wants to speak to our heart.

I make those discoveries through the week in my reading and meditating on Scripture. Immersion in the Word provides the discerning soil. I believe one of the ways we can hone our ability to listen to what the Holy Spirit gives us is by encountering the Holy Spirit through God's Word. The ability to do that is the life of our preaching.

I will read numbers of chapters in both the Old Testament and New Testament. As I do, I look for one thing that slightly interests me or perhaps leaps off the page at me. I will go back to that one verse out of all those chapters, and then for just another five minutes or so meditate on it. I will read it over and over and close my eyes. I'll think about and pray with conviction, "God, get it into me." That combination of Word immersion and prayer is a spiritual digestion process. You take a small piece, bite-size, and chew it over and over. You ask the Holy Spirit to break the nutrients of that Word down and get it into your spiritual bloodstream.

Early in my preaching life I also learned the importance of praying extendedly in the Spirit, sometimes in tongues and sometimes in English as the Spirit led me. I found that even the simple act of praying out loud helped to teach me how to yield verbally to the impulses of the Spirit. Learning to verbalize the heart of the Spirit helped me to overcome my shyness as a communicator.

During my years of preaching, these disciplines have gradually become hardwired into my spiritual discerning process. I keep exercising them regularly. I constantly need to hear God's Spirit through and in the context of His Word. That, to me, is an indispensible backdrop discipline.

As pastors, we need that revelation. We must speak out of what God reveals to us. A congregation needs a shepherd who is utterly dependent on the Holy Spirit, listening to His voice to identify the divinely intended message for each service. Every Sunday people need to know they have heard from God. Yes, this is the ideal. This is not to say everyone has heard from God when I've preached every Sunday. But we prayerfully aim for that. We keep that sense that something simple, profound and clear will come to us during those hours of preparation.

Then we take what we have received, joyfully share it, and watch as the harvest begins to come in.

4 Your Finest Instrument: A Simple Outline

Contemporary audiences have much less patience for twenty-five minutes of exegesis and explanation followed by five minutes of application than did audiences of a generation or two ago.

If a message is to be focused enough to communicate the theme and application you believe God has put on your heart, you need an outline that is equally focused. Every point in that outline must be consistent with that message's purpose, creating a tool that allows you to keep the purpose intact from the beginning of the message to the end. Your outline should act as a kind of logical straight line between the introduction and the conclusion.

As I travel and hear many preachers, I take special notice of the ones who can maintain the focus, identify the key issues, and follow a singular theme. But even seasoned pulpit communicators run into trouble if their message continues for too long or the purpose becomes unfocused. Usually about two-thirds of the way through such a message, any temptation to meander becomes overpowering. One thought leads to another; in no time, the precision instrument that message once was has become a wildly swinging verbal barrage.

Finding the Effective Path

A good outline should communicate the sermon's central purpose at a glance. Here are your two to five key ideas that get you from point A to point B, introduction to conclusion. You look at that outline and ask yourself, "Is this logically a straight line?"

As soon as I use a word like *logically*, the protests begin to arise. Does logic mean we are not in a position to be anointed by the Spirit? Does a commitment to clear thinking mean we're going to plan our message in human strength alone and do away with inspiration? Certainly not. If the Spirit of God has inspired a text that clearly deals with the subject of contentment, for example, then you want to make sure your outline unpacks those verses and follows that singular theme right to the end.

Your commitment to logical thinking is married to your commitment to the inspiration of Scripture and your belief that the Spirit inspires you to communicate those verses clearly. If you commit yourself to clear, logical communication and to hearing the Spirit, your message should move naturally from introducing the idea and catching people's attention, all the way through your presentation of the text and communicating to your listeners what they should do as a result. Everything hangs on that one purpose and points to that moment of decision.

You may be tempted to delve as deeply as possible into a passage's interpretation, but spending twenty minutes on the exegesis defeats your purpose. If you try to put everything you have learned about a passage during your preparation into your sermon, you will quickly fog over the central purpose. I try to exegete just enough so that the central content—"This really is what the passage says and why"—becomes clear. I need to offer just enough of the meaning to identify that central purpose—"This is why we need to think this way, believe this way, act this way, do this thing." Your goal in a purpose-focused message is to offer your listeners actionable takeaways. Your goal is not to give a hermeneutical lesson to them, nor is it just to give them a biblical lesson on every Greek word in that text.

Pruning Your Concept

Depending on your speaking environment, you may offer your focus in different ways. On Wednesday night, I'll take more time to read the text through, verse by verse. It's more of a Bible study venue. However, in reading out the text, I still want to communicate the thread that ties that whole paragraph together.

On Sunday morning when you are dealing with a more general audience, unbelievers are present. You need to work hard ahead of time to find that one purpose and structure the outline so that you quickly communicate the central idea. You don't want people to pick and choose among a variety of themes and wonder, "Well, what do I walk away with here? He said this and he said that." This is especially critical for those with a weak biblical background or with none at all.

In order to create a truly focused outline, you must be willing to edit yourself. I will take what appears to be a completed outline and look for ways to cut 25 percent out of it. It's a tortuous process, because this is stuff you desperately want to say. But when you honestly evaluate your initial effort, you begin to recognize similar points you can group together. You discover ways to save a little time and get the same idea across. It's like pruning a favorite plant in order to encourage growth.

This pruning is very important to me despite the painful process. When I first started University Church in Minneapolis, I preached fifty minutes, fifty-five sometimes. When I pastored Central Assembly, I had trimmed that to thirty to thirty-five minutes. You don't think you can shorten anything you have poured your prayer and creativity into, but if I were to preach pastorally again, I'd cut my Sunday messages down to twenty-three to twenty-eight minutes.

In my pruning, I inevitably discover residual deadweight. I have found that even after I have worked out what I thought was a good outline, I am still sneaking material in there that I don't absolutely need to say. If I am to remain on purpose and see the results I want to see in people's lives, that material simply must go. When I discipline myself to honestly evaluate what appears to be a finished outline and make the hard choices to cut it by 25 percent in length, number of points, and content, I create the tool I need. I am surprised how often, when I finally commit to that process, that I find things I would have said but really did not need to say.

Our emotions and our passions can get the best of us. We tend to paint the most favorable light on every idea we have and believe we can download into people's lives far more material than they can absorb. Part of the simplifying process is to consciously edit out anything peripheral and focus on that which is central to accomplishing the purpose of that message.

That doesn't mean the material is a total waste. When I simplify,

I can save what I cut and store it topically. Nothing prevents me from going back to it and using that material later. Sometimes it makes it easier to sharpen an outline if I know I am just setting aside good stuff rather than throwing it away.

You have one focus, one singular purpose, but it doesn't mean you have only one point in your sermon. There may be different nuances. I may be giving a message on marriage, and unpacking Ephesians 5 where Paul talks about mutual submission between wives and husbands. There are different nuances of what it means to meet each other's needs as a husband and wife. There may be two or three application statements. But when it is all said and done, I am still sticking to one subject. As I go through the different verses, I can also offer applications that connect with a broad cross-section of marriages in my congregation. A singular, simple purpose doesn't mean you only get to connect with one or two people and be irrelevant to everyone else.

Designing Application Statements

Many of us grew up listening to sermon outlines with propositional outline statements—A. Jesus Is Love; B. Jesus Is Lord, etc. Much of the preaching I listened to growing up followed that three-point, propositional delivery. The problem is, that format requires the listener to distill personal application from your message over the long haul. At some level, everyone present is asking the question, "Why should I be giving you a half-hour of my life to listen to what you have to say?" The answer to that question should be concrete and applicational, and you need to offer that answer as soon as possible.

There needs to be a "Hey you!" element early on to get their attention and help them to see how your message is going to hit their life.

I pastored near Saddleback Church in Southern California. I know Pastor Rick Warren has his critics, but I clearly saw that church's impact on the greater community. Thousands of people radically committed themselves to Christ. Contrary to what some critics claim, in Warren's effort to communicate with seekers and unbelievers he does not water things down. He is very biblical and very in-your-face when it comes to what you need to do in response to the Word.

I attended one of Warren's preaching seminars. "If application is the point," he taught us, "make the points application." If application is the point of your message, transform your outline points into application statements. Take your outline, take out the passive verbs, and structure each key statement around something that the audience relates to or must do. This may not be realistic for every main point in your outline, but it should be your goal.

To go back to my example above, rather than placing "Jesus Is Love" as your first point, you might direct an application question at the audience: "Have you ever been loved unconditionally?" or "Have you ever doubted God's love for you?" Instead of "Jesus Is Lord," you could say, "Here are some places where we tend to shut God out," or ask, "Where in your life are you avoiding Jesus?" You are still presenting lordship issues, you're still packaging Jesus' identity in an accessible manner, but you're making the material much more applicational. You're bringing application to the forefront and supporting it with Scripture as you go.

You may need to do some exegesis on a passage. You may need to define a Greek word. You may need to give some historical context. However, rather than doing that all up front and then explaining the application in the last few minutes of the message, imbed application in the core structure of the outline.

Contemporary audiences have much less patience for twenty-five minutes of exegesis and explanation followed by five minutes of application than did audiences of a generation or two ago. Build the outline and then turn the declarative, propositional points of that outline into applicational statements supported by the text and linked by the central purpose.

If you go into some deep exploration of the text, it might be interesting to you, but you might also be losing your crowd. Someone out there may be about to lose his or her job. Someone else may have a kid who ran away from home. So, as you go through the structure of that message, you must answer not only the "What?" of the text, but the "So what?" of how it connects with their lives.

Application issues should engage people, connect their life with your message, and help them know what to understand and what to do. Application points need to be practical. And they need to be doable. They can't be unrealistic; they can't be too idealistic or theoretical. Realistic application connects with people and contributes to the kind of reduced, streamlined, straight-lined outlines you need for effectiveness.

Keeping Scripture at the Center

You need a central focus. You need application points. But, most of all, you need the life of God's Word worked into every cell of the body of your sermon. Support every key point you make with Scripture. Keep referring to Scripture throughout the message.

Visiting a church, I listened to the pastor preach a good message that was probably forty minutes long. It was a specific, topical message. However, he read the Scripture passage only once, at the beginning, and he never actually read the text again. Finally, toward the end of his message, I realized, "Oh, those were the four points in the Scripture," but he had never referred back to the text during the body of the message. It made the message hard to follow because there were no ongoing references to the Scripture passage itself.

You can get a congregation's attention. You can demonstrate how your biblical theme applies to their lives. You can call them to practical action. But if your message fails to actually look at the Scripture text, all you have is a good motivational talk. Your exploration of the Word needs to pull your listeners in with you. Have them read the verses with you in their Bible, or project them for everyone to see and read together. If they are coming to church, they want to know what the Bible says. No matter how contemporary your preaching is, it is never old-fashioned or irrelevant to actually have people look at the text of the Scripture.

Keep referring to Scripture throughout the message and, especially, support every key point with Scripture.

Adding Depth

A way to add depth to the message is to ask the question, "Why?" I call this the bridge question between "What?" and "So what?" Consider a simple message on Jesus teaching us to love our neighbors. As you read the Scripture to the audience, engage them in the question, "Why would Jesus teach that?"

Buddhism, for example, seeks to purge human passion, including love. So, why would God say to love each other? There might be a real advantage to purging ourself of all kinds of passion. If Mother's going to take care of me, why should I try to take care of other people? Sometimes, not only "What does the text say and mean?" but also "Why does that make sense?" helps us to engage the Word.

When I was preparing a message on contentment, I started thinking, "What's the difference between contentment and complacency?" I had never heard anybody talk about the difference. I didn't want people to settle for complacency thinking it was contentment. Complacency has no passion for missions, complacency has no need for faith, and complacency has no tolerance for sacrifice. That's all very different from contentment. I kept asking myself the "why" question. Why is contentment important, and how is it different from complacency? Sometimes, a key question makes people who have heard a passage of Scripture for years feel more "fed" because you are really helping them dig deeper into the Word and think through important questions.

Trusting the Spirit

I mentioned earlier the importance of clear, logical thinking in your message preparation. And I emphasized that such thinking is never intended to compromise your interaction with the Holy Spirit. You develop a purpose and embed it in your application points. You keep at the forefront of your attention the effect your message will have on people's lives. At all times, you are seeking a simple structure with clear points people need to understand and things they need to do. You want to draw them right in from the start and repeatedly expose them to the content of God's Word.

Every part of the above task is perfectly in line with what the Holy Spirit wants to accomplish in each member of the body of Christ. When the Holy Spirit is working, He can take that Word and shape it. To use an aeronautical expression, He can actually "land it," as the Lord once put it to me. *You let it fly*, I have sensed God say to me more than once during my message preparation, *and I'll land it.* The Spirit knows how to land that key thought right where people may be in their life at that point. He can also use that simple application to touch broad spheres in people's lives. The Holy Spirit is always at work in people's lives and always has a divinely planned intersection between your message and people's hearts.

To see that divine imprint most clearly on my message, I must intentionally interact with the Spirit. I study the text and then pace while I pray in the Spirit. I meditate on the central purpose I envision for the message, praying earnestly and repeatedly, "Lord, what is it that You want to say?" For many texts, there are multiple directions I could legitimately go to make applications. But in prayer, I'm asking God to identify what should take place behind His pulpit that day. "What is it that You really want to say to these people this week?" We have to exegete not only the text but what God is doing spiritually among His people and in their lives.

The Holy Spirit does not ask us to operate in a relational

vacuum. The pastor's study is not his or her castle. The Spirit works relationally, and so too must pastors as they bring the Word to life. Even though I have sometimes pastored large churches, I kept an afternoon or two a week available just to talk to people. Anyone who wanted to could come in and spend time with me. Those individual relationships always enriched my message by keeping me connected with real people.

My responsibility is not just to preach a good sermon. Ultimately, no matter how eloquently I vocalize my outline, it's not a good message unless God's Spirit speaks specifically to real issues in people's lives. The Spirit must awaken their understanding. The Spirit must lead them into action.

5 Filling In Your Outline

People aren't there to give you a chance to preach. You are there to be God's mouthpiece into their lives.

I once heard Dr. George O. Wood's preaching characterized this way: He says predictable things in unpredictable ways. There are countless predictable things we can teach from Scripture. We are all using the same Book for our primary source. But when we present scriptural truth in a creative and unexpected manner, we capture our audience's attention. Dr. Wood has a way of phrasing well-known truths from the Word in ways that are concise and creative.

A pastor rarely has a homogeneous audience. Multiple generations come to a church with a spectrum of life experiences. You need to find ways to feed the saint who has heard your text for fifty years as well as the person who is sitting in church that day for the very first time. You can capture both people if you avoid predictability for the saint and clearly create life connections for that new person.

Flesh Out Your "Skeleton"

Once you have developed a focused outline that is sensitized and simplified to communicate a specific truth and meet a specific need, you then want to develop your key points. You should already have created points that relate to real issues in people's lives rather than merely stating impersonal propositions. In other words, the points are applicational. But sometimes your key points need to be reduced in length and reworded to become more memorable and understandable.

This doesn't apply to every point, but at times you can discern a certain rhythm. Perhaps each point starts with the same letter. Perhaps they form an acrostic. Forcing every point to fit into an artificial pattern can tempt you to be unfair with the text, but you may want to rephrase the points so that they are more memorable.

For example, you may develop a theme such as, "Here are the most important aspects of a successful life." You might reduce that to say, "How to love life" or "How to love living." If it feels awkward to say a point out loud, it will probably be awkward for your audience to remember. You want to develop applicational truth statements that nurture audience interest and memorization. Stronger verbs accomplish this more readily than passive verbs. A colorful adjective can fulfill this purpose as long as you don't cross the line and try to sound artificial or sensational. When you word your points carefully, you create a message that will seal itself into the memory of the listener.

Illustrate your key points. Use real-life examples, even visual aids if possible. Analogies and illustrations are windows to truth. These can be as simple as a quick "for example" statement, or stretch into a more detailed story. Contemporary audiences will more readily respond to a challenge when you couch it as a story rather than a confrontation. Our culture says, "Love me but don't judge me." Telling a story allows you to slip between the barriers that a resistant audience will raise to the truth. Rather than bluntly proclaiming what people ought to do, stories and illustrations allow you to diplomatically and effectively communicate truth to be acted on. Our postmodern culture requires us to return to Jesus' teaching methods. Rather than orating "shoulds" and "ought tos" at people, we can tell compelling stories that illustrate how someone actually embodied that in life.

Your Sunday morning audience most likely includes older people, young people, fairly poor people and fairly wealthy people. You have married people and unmarried people. How do you embrace that kind of diversity? When I preach, I take into consideration the different people I am serving. Everybody loves a good story. I aim at my younger audience to draw them in, but keep in mind every age group. I always thought it was a great compliment to a message if a parent told me, "You know, my fourteen-year-old kid takes notes and really likes what you say." I may have PhDs and seminary teachers sitting in the crowd, but if I can connect with that fourteen-year-old and say something meaningful out of the text and tell a relatable story, it will also connect with the rest of the audience.

Stories can be supplemented at times with visuals. You might simply hold up a solid object to illustrate a more symbolic truth. You might use a quick video clip.

Invite Participation

I like to project notes during my Sunday morning message. I leave blank spaces in key statements so people can fill in the right word when I get to it in the printed outline. Many people are not primarily auditory learners. So, anything you can do visually increases their capacity to learn and remember.

Sometimes, you might encourage the congregation to interact with the point. Participation can be as basic as saying a word out loud or repeating a phrase after you. You don't want to overuse that tool because it gets very old if you do it more than once or twice in a message. And you don't want to take that tack in every sermon. With today's technology, you can also ask the people to text an answer to a question that's too involved. People are texting anyway while you preach, so you might as well face that reality and get them texting to you and interacting with the message.

Reading Scripture at the beginning of the message or a key Scripture during the message offers interactive potential. I'll say, "Let's read that Scripture out loud." I might have the verses in notes I've handed out or on the screen or take the more traditional approach of directing those present to the passage in their Bible. But I don't assume that everyone who comes Sunday morning is familiar with God's Word. That's why I'll put Scripture verses in notes and on the screen—so some people don't begin to feel the message is not for them because they don't know their way around the Bible.

Visual aids should never replace a message's core substance. They should illustrate and accentuate, not distract. If these secondary tools supplant the substance of the message or substitute for the hard work of exegeting the text, they lose their value. You must continue to wrestle with your outline and make sure it grabs people where they are, relates to them, draws them in and communicates correctly the illuminating truth of God's Word for their life. Visuals can also be counterproductive if they are too long. If I use a video clip in a sermon, the video will last no longer than three minutes max and will usually be the only one used in that particular message.

Control Pacing and Transitions

A message needs the correct pacing. How long do I spend on certain points? Am I giving the most time to the central truths, or does a subpoint with an illustration stretch too long? I need to move through points fairly quickly so the flow of the message is not compromised and so that people come away with a solid overview of what I have taught. That is all part of pacing.

Pacing also helps you to avoid the unending crescendo. Try graphing the intensity of your message. I look at my points and take note of where the content is quite focused and intense. That calls for what I call a "psychological space" where people can relax and catch their breath a moment before the next point. Psychological space is a good place for a story or perhaps some humor. I never want to compromise the impact of the message. But people periodically need an opportunity to regain some emotional equilibrium. We can all afford to laugh at ourself after a punch in the gut with the truth, or at least experience a moment when the intensity eases.

Transitions between points need special attention and are very awkward if you haven't answered the question, "What's the one thing

I'm speaking about here?" Your central theme helps you move from point to point, and keeps transitions from becoming rabbit trails. Sometimes it's as simple as, "So, in order to develop a generous lifestyle, the second thing we can do is . . .". A story might serve as the transition. You might pose a question: "Have you ever wondered . . .?" Good transitions are vital to the flow of your message.

As pacing and transitions take final form in the outline, your message begins to sound like a story. One point raises the next point, a sense of connection between text and needs continually draws people in, and your audience begins to grasp the life application for which you are aiming. I try to phrase the application statement personally and then take people to the text and show them how it comes out of the text.

Again, balance is the key. Don't take twenty minutes exegeting the text, explaining its historical background and laying out the schematics—all the things that are fascinating to us as biblical teachers—and then use just five or ten minutes in application at the end. Your average junior high student is not going to stick with you that long. Even your average sixty-five-year-olds will be tempted to let their minds wander after a while.

Answer Questions

Here is a valuable final check for your outline: "Is this really addressing the real questions people have, the real issues they face in life?" People aren't there to give you a chance to preach. You are there to be God's mouthpiece into their lives.

People come to church expecting answers to their toughest

questions. Your ministry, over the long term, needs to grapple with the spectrum of life questions we all encounter. No, you won't answer every question to the same degree or to everyone's satisfaction. But your messages need to illuminate scriptural life application in a way that gives direction for your congregation as they are working through their own faith walk.

Depending on their background, people have different expectations of a pastor. Churched evangelicals develop a high sense of anxiety with ambiguity. When a subject doesn't have a clear black-and-white simplistic answer, they can get nervous. Unchurched people, on the other hand, will probably respect you for being honest with what is answerable and what is not answerable.

Prayerfully direct your attention to your congregation's needs and help people come to grips with their questions from a position of confidence in God's Word, even when the black-and-white solution does not present itself. Give the best answers you can. At all times, put yourself in the position of your listeners.

In dealing with questions arising from a given text, be careful to avoid minor queries that distract from the central theme. Many questions can develop from historical minutiae or out of commentators' disagreement over the interpretation of little-used words in the original languages. "This Hebrew expression only appears here and in two other passages of Scripture and its meaning is unclear." Rarely do minor or specialized questions help a person deal with a crisis or season of doubt.

As with other areas of your study and preparation, dealing with questions is a balancing act. You really need the Spirit's guidance and wisdom in this process. Prayerfully seek His direction.

Listen and Learn

I came to a point in ministry when I struggled to anticipate people's questions related to a given text in Scripture. This is when I developed the informal sermon evaluation committee I described in chapter 1 to help me deal with this challenge. As I would listen to their evaluation of past messages, I gained insight in preparing future material.

Bringing people into my inner circle of critics nurtured my humility. As you invite others to evaluate your pulpit ministry, you will experience a humbling infusion of strength. If your ego is too wired into your ownership of your material, you won't get the feedback that can really help you to improve.

I suspect a lot of interpersonal conflict between pastors and parishioners could be avoided through this process. When you structure feedback opportunities and ask for others' input humbly, people are far less likely to be vicious or mean-spirited or hurtful to you. On the other hand, when they desperately need to say something to you and your ego is creating a barrier to their input, people tend to become more forceful. Invite feedback humbly. Evaluation is painful, but when you check your ego at the Cross, it can only help you grow.

Take the time also to listen to your own messages. I do that periodically and find it to be a very difficult experience, but one that helps me become a better communicator. Idiosyncrasies, artificial phrasing or emotions, distracting minor subjects—all of this and more—become apparent when you honestly evaluate yourself. I also make a habit of listening to great communicators in order to learn from them.

In the end, it is God who accomplishes the desired life-change from our messages by His Spirit through His truth—in spite of our bumbling. We need to do our best, but our best is never good enough in and of itself. God is our Source. He can help us preach and teach Scripture in ways that engage people's minds, emotions and wills. And, He is the One who actually speaks through us as we communicate His Word in the power of His Spirit.

Conclusion

We've come to the end of our journey. I want to challenge you to assess where you are in ministry, where the Holy Spirit would have you to go, and how the principles in these chapters can come to life in your church. Are you satisfied with what you are doing? More importantly, is the Lord satisfied? Are you willing to do something about it?

Nothing I have shared in these pages is unduly complicated. But much time, effort, and prayer are needed if you want to put this book into practice. If you are a bivocational pastor with a small or nonexistent staff, that can feel overwhelming. And yet, even small steps in the direction we have considered will bring great spiritual returns.

Ask yourself, "If somebody hears me preach for five years, what are they going to look like at the end of five years?" Be very intentional with that question. Realize that what you share every Sunday morning when you preach must be the authentic Word of the Lord. You are called to educate people in the knowledge of Scripture, engage them at a spiritually passionate level, and present the Word in a manner that constantly directs their life choices.

I would encourage you, wherever you believe yourself to be in this transformational process, to begin setting aside more time to make possible the changes you have identified as necessary. You might begin by adding an hour or two a week into your sermon preparation. Six months from now, you could begin looking for another hour. What happens in that Sunday message is powerfully indicative of the growth of your church, the growth of the people, and their vitality in ministry.

The Sunday morning message and what you're doing during the week with leadership development will help you to grow your leadership team and begin to off-load some responsibilities as you build leaders. Determine to incrementally move from where you are to the next level.

I pastored four very different churches—Christians in Action University Church in Minneapolis, Minnesota; Newport-Mesa in Southern California; Broadway Pentecostal Church in Vancouver, Canada; and Central Assembly in Springfield, Missouri. Each church came with its own unique dynamics. Each stretched me personally and spiritually. I pray that I accomplished all that God envisioned for my ministry with each of those congregations.

You're not going to find one more minute in your week next week than you had this week or last week. You won't find time to change; you will have to take time. To take time, you will have to take it away from something else and say, "This is a higher priority."

When I was pastoring young adults at University Church, my one-on-one counseling load was overwhelming. It felt like everyone was dealing with life identity issues, relationship issues, or life direction issues. I decided I needed to spend more time training leaders. Once we developed small groups where the leaders were trained to really disciple the people in their groups, my counseling load dropped by half.

Even when I was pastoring in Southern California, a much larger church, my week could fill up just seeing people. People wanted to come and talk about their life. I finally began to discern that I was hurting the whole congregation by spending too much time one-on-one. I had a heart for individual people, a kind of mercy gift that way, but I also recognized my larger responsibility. I realized I could spend hours trying to help one person, or invest more hours in scriptural teaching that would help everybody. Paul Lowenberg, my father-in-law, was a great preacher. He said, "I like to think I'm counseling in my preaching."

Remember, you are called as a minister to equip your people to do the work of the ministry as well. It's not about your doing everything. Your church will be newly energized as you seek change on two fronts. Always work to raise up leaders to off-load elements of your church's ministry handprint. Then take the corresponding time to spend more time in message preparation. You will begin to give your most precious resource, time, to one of your highest priorities—preaching.

About James Bradford

James (Jim) Bradford was elected general secretary of the Assemblies of God by the Executive Presbytery in February 2009. He is a member of the Executive Leadership Team and the Executive Presbytery. As general secretary, Jim oversees the credentialing of ministers, church chartering, the collection of official statistics, the Flower Pentecostal Heritage Center, Ministerial Resourcing and the Network for Women in Ministry.

Prior to his election as general secretary, Jim served as senior pastor of Central Assembly in Springfield, Missouri. Jim holds a PhD in aerospace engineering from the University of Minnesota. As a student he led a small Chi Alpha campus Bible study that eventually grew into a university church. Upon graduation in 1979, Jim stepped into full-time ministry with that campus outreach. In 1988, Jim and his family moved to Southern California where he pastored Newport-Mesa Christian Center in the heart of Orange County.

Twelve years later, he transitioned to Vancouver, British Columbia, to pastor Broadway Church. It was in 2003 that Jim and his family moved to Springfield to assume the pastorate of Central Assembly.

Bradford has also served on a variety of executive boards including that of Vanguard University, the Southern California District Executive Presbytery, and the General Presbytery of the Assemblies of God.

Bradford and his wife, Sandi, have two grown daughters, Meredith and Angeline.